The Great Depression
and World War II:
Organizing America, 1933–1945

The Great Depression and World War II: Organizing America, 1933–1945

GERALD D. NASH

University of New Mexico

Under the General Editorship
of Vincent P. Carosso

St. Martin's Press
New York

To Marie and Stephanie

Library of Congress Catalog Card Number: 78-65209
Copyright © 1979 by St. Martin's Press, Inc.
All Rights Reserved.
Manufactured in the United States of America.
32109
fedcb
For information, write St. Martin's Press, Inc.
175 Fifth Avenue, New York, N.Y. 10010
cover design: Pat Vitacco
cloth ISBN: 0-312-34561-5
paper ISBN: 0-312-34562-3

Preface

My chief purpose in this volume is to help students understand the
lasting impact on the American people of the Great Depression and
World War II—to recognize that the two events irrevocably altered
the political, economic, social, and cultural life of the nation. I have
sought to accomplish this objective by providing a brief, succinct nar-
rative of the years between 1933 and 1945 and by examining how the
major events of the period accelerated the growth of an organizational
society in the United States. The crises of depression and war stimulated the expansion of both governmental and corporate bureaucracy
and paved the way for the dominance, in American society, of giant
public and private institutions.

During the nineteenth century, Americans had felt that the individual could respond to most of the challenges posed by what was then
a predominantly rural society; in the urbanized, technological civilization of the twentieth century, their faith in individualism waned. They
began to place increasing confidence in organizations staffed by specialists to deal with the complexities of an industrialized nation.
Between 1933 and 1945 they authorized government to assume
unprecedented powers; at the same time, they supported the
emergence of the corporation as the dominant institution in the private
sector. The man who governed the nation during this period of
upheaval and change embodied both the nineteenth- and twentieth-
century strands of the American experience. If Franklin D. Roosevelt

was an individualist at heart, the circumstances of his time led him to crystallize and broaden the organizational structure of American society.

As the New Deal and the war resulted in the expansion of government and business, so they intensified the drive for collective action among the country's underrepresented groups. I have endeavored to show that the reaffirmation of the nation's social, political, and economic integrity depended upon the participation of minorities—blacks, Hispanics, Jews, Native-Americans—and women. In the minds of Roosevelt and other New Dealers, national recovery was closely linked to the lessening of racial, religious, and ethnic hostility. The war, in turn, proved to be a time of both disruption and increased opportunity for the deprived and the excluded. Mobilization created a multitude of jobs; but as blacks and others streamed into the cities, the result was, frequently, overcrowded housing, inadequate educational and recreational facilities, and the kindling of tension between newly arrived blacks and ethnic communities that had come to the cities as emigrants from abroad a generation before. But the organizational strength attained by the various groups abided and continued to assert itself.

My perspective on the period between 1933 and 1945 derives in part from the research conducted, during the 1970s, by a group of organizational historians. Taking their cue from the great German sociologist Max Weber and other pioneering social scientists, the organizational historians have focused on the rise of bureaucracy in the twentieth century as one of the salient characteristics of an increasingly technological world. The studies of Robert Wiebe, Ellis W. Hawley, Alfred D. Chandler, Louis Galambos, Robert D. Cuff, Richard Polenberg, and others have touched upon particular phases of the growth of organizations. Their works—and other specialized works of sociologists and economists—have provided the theoretical context in which I have presented a crucial era in American history.

In the completion of the volume I have incurred debts too numerous to mention. I owe special gratitude to Professor Vincent P. Carosso of New York University, the editor of this series, for his unfailing encouragement, wise counsel, and trust. He has been both mentor and friend. The staff of St. Martin's Press provided able help at every stage in the preparation of this work and made it a pleasurable experience. Mrs. Edith Jonas gave valuable research aid. My family bore my distractions with the New Deal and the Second World War patiently and good-humoredly. Although many individuals contributed to the final product, I bear sole responsibility for its substance and interpretations.

GERALD D. NASH

Contents

Editor's Introduction

In less than a generation, the twentieth century will belong entirely to the past. Many of the great personalities and events of the first half of the century already seem remote. To Americans born after World War II and to many others as well, Theodore Roosevelt is little more than a name and a picture in a history book, a bespectacled president with a mustache and a broad and toothy grin. Few people living today remember the young, dynamic Roosevelt—the popular hero of San Juan Hill, the first president to visit a foreign country (Panama) during his term of office and to ride in an automobile. And, indeed, the America of TR's day has all but disappeared.

Since 1901, when Roosevelt assumed the presidency, urbanization and industrialization have wrought profound changes in the United States. At the turn of the century the population was 76 million. Fewer than 40 percent lived in urban areas of 2,500 or more; and although American cities were growing rapidly, only six had a population of a half-million or more, and only three had reached or surpassed a million. In 1900, for the first time, the number of industrial wage earners exceeded the number of farmers and farm laborers, and the value of manufactured goods produced by the nation's workers was more than twice the $4.7 billion attributed to agriculture. The loosely organized, largely agricultural country of less than a half-century earlier was on the way to becoming a tightly integrated, highly industrialized, urban nation. But the road would be far from smooth or straight, and American society would experience unalterable changes over the next eight decades.

By 1970 the nation's population had grown to 205 million, and nearly 74 percent of the people had come to live in cities and their ever-expanding suburbs. Urbanization had changed the face of America, creating vast new metropolitan areas that linked city upon city into huge megalopolises, or "urban conglomerates." Similarly, the continued growth of big business transformed the economic landscape. The United States Steel Corporation, founded in 1901, was the country's first billion-dollar firm; by 1970 over a hundred such corporate leviathans existed. Only a few businesses in 1900 commanded a national market; in the 1970s large corporate enterprises dominated nearly every sector of the nation's economy, and many of these giants exercised increasing might abroad. Industrialism also helped alter the nation's international status. In 1900 the United States, despite its recently acquired overseas possessions, was still a new power of limited influence outside the Western Hemisphere. Following World War II it became one of the two superpowers.

But power, like industrial leadership—the twin developments hailed by many at the turn of the century as signaling the beginning of a new era in the nation—made other observers uneasy. The steady growth of large businesses, the rapidly expanding cities, and increased involvement in international affairs would inevitably create vast changes in American life. Turn-of-the-century commentators and politicians focused on many of the central issues that have faced the American people ever since: how to adapt institutions and policies to the needs of an industrial society; how to protect the environment while promoting material progress; how to provide an equitable and humane judicial system; how to deal with racial and ethnic diversity; how to preserve the nation's security in an increasingly turbulent world and contribute, at the same time, to international peace and stability. The four volumes in this series present America's attempts to respond to such challenges.

Professor Gerald Nash's work, the third volume in the chronological sequence, treats the years of the nation's worst depression and its costliest war, a period during which one man—Franklin D. Roosevelt—stamped his character and personality, his ideals and hopes, on an entire decade and, in the process, came to hold a virtual monopoly on the country's political leadership. For a dozen years America looked to him, first to pull it out of a searing depression, then to lead it to victory over intransigent enemies across two oceans. Roosevelt's indomitable spirit, his contagious self-confidence and optimism, served as a tonic to a nation yearning for leadership and action. His programs to restore and reform the economic system produced what Nash calls "a whole galaxy of new laws" of wide and lasting significance. To be sure, some of the president's programs fell considerably short of their objectives, and Nash is careful to point out where and why the New Deal failed—as well as where and how it succeeded.

Not the least important feature of the New Deal was a wholly unintended by-product, one which the president himself deplored: the growth and institutionalization of a depersonalized, organizational society, in which self-reliance and self-sufficiency yielded to increasing dependency on the initiatives of large groups—big business, big farm associations, big unions, big government. Though Roosevelt was, as Nash indicates, neither an "organization man" nor an especially tidy administrator, his years in the White House witnessed a huge expansion of the federal bureaucracy and the triumph of large institutional structures in every sector of American life. The long, deep Depression, the demands for greater economic security and social justice, the upheaval of global war—these were the reasons for the plethora of administrative agencies spawned by the New Deal. For even before the new organizational structure had achieved its dual purpose—to restore and reform an economically scarred society—a militant totalitarianism appeared in Europe and Asia and soon threatened the nation's security. The machinery that Roosevelt had created to fight the Depression had to be adapted and expanded to prepare the country to defeat the challenges posed by fascism and militarism.

This volume tells the story of the New Deal's twelve years of almost continual crisis, a time of intense controversy and enduring political, social, and economic change. Nash covers these years of high drama dispassionately; his judgments, based on both extensive reading and his own mature insights, are balanced and judicious. Here, then, in compact form, the reader will find the essence of the New Deal era, clearly and interestingly told.

VINCENT P. CAROSSO

CHAPTER 1

American Society in Crisis

With his vision of a "New Day," Herbert Hoover hoped to attract the attention of Americans—and their votes. In 1928 the Great Engineer's promise to eradicate poverty seemed eminently plausible, even if it was but a crude approximation of the American Dream. Most Americans had just lived through an amazing decade in which they witnessed significant change in many aspects of American life, including Hoover's accomplishments in social welfare.

The promise of the 1920s was a higher living standard for a majority of Americans. In many ways the decade was a harbinger of the Affluent Society that emerged in the United States after World War II. Although most people realized during the 1920s that the abolition of want still lay in the future, nevertheless the prosperity of that decade encouraged a mood of upbeat optimism among millions. Certainly the vision of affluence was based on sound considerations. During this period American industry developed mass production techniques that permitted the creation of vast quantities of goods at low prices. In a way Henry Ford's huge, new River Rouge plant near Detroit was a symbol of this new order. Along with mass production, American business revolutionized large-scale distribution of consumer items through such devices as more sophisticated advertising, installment buying plans, and chain stores. Corporations now issued stock publicly on an extensive scale, and millions of individuals acquired shares in huge American business enterprises. The material well-being of many Americans improved, while the average work week was significantly reduced in many industries from fifty to forty-five hours. In the 1920s the dreams of the average man or woman appeared within reach. The eradication of poverty seemed possible, and a new age of material affluence was close at hand.

THE SEARCH FOR ORDER: GROWTH OF AN ORGANIZATIONAL SOCIETY, 1917–1932

The search for order and stability began in the late nineteenth century in the increasingly chaotic and insecure world ushered in by the age of industrialism. That search was to dominate Americans throughout the course of the twentieth century as they sought to achieve the elusive goal of economic and social stability. The generation of the 1920s contributed much to this effort by fashioning building blocks that would lay the foundations of the organizational society in twentieth-century America. Using the ideas and experiences of the Progressive Era and World War I, they reorganized their economy, every level of government, many aspects of their social and cultural life, and their diplomacy. The process often was not deliberate, but rather, was a pragmatic response to immediate problems. Nor was the extent of this reorganization always clearly apparent to those who lived through it. If between 1933 and 1945 Americans responded positively to Franklin D. Roosevelt's call for help in coping with the problems of depression and global war, however, their acquiescence was not really due to a sudden conversion on their part. Their experiences from 1917 to 1932 had predisposed them to think and act within the framework of organizational imperatives in the pursuit of stability and order.

A distinctive characteristic of the technologically oriented mass production and distribution economy of the 1920s was the formation of organizations designed to minimize economic risks and to prevent destructive competition, competition based on unfair business methods. Trade associations, which mushroomed during the decade, reflected these efforts. Their functions ranged from attempts at price maintenance, sharing and disseminating useful information, and regulating competition to lobbying at local, state, or national government levels. Large American corporations such as DuPont or General Motors joined international cartels to control the production and distribution of particular products on an industry-wide basis. The proliferation of new federal agencies and increased regulatory activity on the part of the Federal Trade Commission, as well as the expanded activities of the Department of Commerce, were another reflection of the efforts to stabilize the highly competitive business world.

Similar trends characterized American agriculture. Caught in the throes of the Depression, most farmers abandoned some of their once-vaunted individualism to embrace organization as a key to greater prosperity and security. Like businessmen they formed their own protective associations such as the American Farm Bureau Federation and the Farmers' Union, which lobbied for farm causes at various levels of government. Through the expansion of agricultural cooperatives and similar organizations, farmers tried unsuccessfully to achieve a more favorable balance between what they produced and what they could profitably market. They sought to stabilize farm prices and to increase their margin of profit. Low-cost credit, granted by the Federal Intermediate Credit Bank system created in 1923; and the purchasing of farm surpluses to maintain agricultural price levels, authorized under the Agricultural Marketing Act of 1929, were attempts to find support from the government.

To a lesser extent workers also tried to organize themselves more effectively to secure stable wage levels and improved working conditions. Strong opposition from business and various decisions of the U.S. Supreme Court, however, led to little success on the part of the labor union organizers. Big corporations established company unions as a means of preempting workers from forming independent labor organizations. Such unions were organized and managed by particular business firms. Some of the older and stronger unions such as the railroad workers turned to the federal government for help. The Railroad Labor Act of 1926, for example, imposed an organizational structure on railway labor-management relations by providing for federal mediation in disputes, arbitration, supervision of pension systems, and the maintenance of many of the benefits already secured by railroad workers.

While the 1920s saw the establishment of new organizations designed to minimize the insecurities of an industrial economy and new relationships among government, workers, and business, it also brought on the age of manager and the specialist. In large corporations, farm organizations, or unions, professionals and managers came to exercise a significant amount of power. Herbert Hoover noted this trend when he observed that the United States had entered a "New Era" in which scientific and management experts would apply their particular skills to society's increasingly complex social issues. The special competence of the engineer, Hoover declared, could be used to solve the nation's problems. The term "social engineering" acquired great popularity during the 1920s. Americans who remembered the recent World War I experience, in which centralized management by experts provided the key to victory, enthusiastically embraced the concept. And those who had supported reform movements during the Progressive Era considered efficiency a prime goal, best achieved through organizations staffed by experts.

The organizational urges of Americans in the 1920s also affected racial and ethnic minorities. Sensing accurately that organization would enable them to exert greater influence on American life, millions of ethnic Americans banded together in civic and fraternal groups and formed political organizations. In the eastern and midwestern cities, they constituted large voting blocs, which by 1920, were beginning to wield sufficient power to influence the course of urban politics and to exercise a significant voice in state and national elections. In states such as Massachusetts, New York, Pennsylvania, and Illinois, for example, ethnic minorities began to hold a crucial balance of power. Governor Alfred E. Smith of New York became a spokesman for urban minorities in the 1920s, and through this voter base, won enough support to be nominated as a presidential candidate in 1928.

Thousands of black Americans flocked to the banner of Marcus Garvey, a Jamaican who led a black nationalist movement. Garvey preached about the need for blacks to organize themselves more effectively to combat racial prejudice and discrimination. Native-Americans strove more aggressively for their rights through newly formed groups such as the American Indian Rights Association. Spanish-speaking

Americans banded together in the League of United Latin American Citizens. The consciousness of women was higher in the 1920s than in pre-World War I America, spurred no doubt by their enfranchisement in 1920.

Such increasing awareness of ethnic and racial minorities and their effort to expand their economic and social status in American society was reflected in American politics during these years. Native-born, rural Americans saw their power wane as urban, immigrant Americans achieved positions of political influence. This trend was reflected in the growth of an urban coalition in the Democratic Party. Until World War I the nucleus of the Democrats' power was in the South, but between 1920 and 1932 the prime base of their support moved to the large cities of the East and Midwest. During this period the Democrats attracted the immigrant masses of the urban centers, an increasing number of blacks, and large numbers of blue collar workers. As political analyst Samuel Lubell noted, by 1928 this shift of political power in America was virtually completed. Somewhat more insecure than native born Americans who formed the core of Republican strength, the urban Democratic coalition looked to the federal government to maintain stability and order.

Cultural life in the 1920s also was affected by the emphasis on organization. A new age of mass culture emerged. This was the heyday of organized spectator sports, particularly major league baseball and prize fighting. Babe Ruth and Jack Dempsey were better known to many Americans than were leading businessmen or politicians. It was also the Golden Age of the silent film. Fifty million Americans went to the movies each week to follow the exploits of such stars as Rudolph Valentino or Clara Bow. Millions tuned in their radio sets to listen to programs beamed over the new national radio networks such as NBC. The circulation of mass-oriented magazines, of which *True Story* was an example, boomed in the 1920s. Improvement of recording techniques provided a new means for the mass distribution and popularization of all forms of music by record companies such as RCA Victor, and scores of others. Entertainment—once largely provided by family and friends—now was packaged by large organizations.

Periods of rapid change in a society invariably lead to a questioning of traditional values. During the 1920s the Protestant ethic came under increasing attack as the writers of the Lost Generation spearheaded an assault on the traditional values revered by many Americans before the First World War. Not only in literature, but also in art, music, and philosophy, traditionalism was derided as being out of step with the new winds of change. American intellectuals were fragmented during the period as the conflict between traditionalists and nontraditionalists destroyed whatever consensus on cultural values Americans once held. The nineteenth-century system of values was beginning to disintegrate under twentieth-century pressures.

In foreign affairs as in domestic life, Americans sought stability and order. Although the United States did not assume the major responsibilities for world leadership that membership in the League of Nations entailed, neither did the nation retreat into extreme isolation. America's presence was felt around the globe. The United States worked informally with the League of Nations, played a major role in settling war debt and reparations problems via the Dawes (1924) and Young (1929) plans, and initiated the Kellogg-Briand Pact (1928) to outlaw war. The treaties arising out of the Washington Conference of 1921 were designed to impose an American-oriented balance of power in the Far East. United States policies regarding Latin America were designed to build a system of hemispheric solidarity that would no longer require direct military intervention. The State Department professionalized its staff during the decade and formed a corps of professional diplomats as specialized and competent as the managers of large business corporations.

Between World War I and the eve of the Great Depression, then, Americans had opted for increased organization as a means of coping with the many problems of their rapidly changing society brought on by the industrial age. The pace of this organizational growth was to be greatly accelerated, however, by the Great Depression.

THE COLLAPSE OF AMERICAN SOCIETY

Within a few months of the Great Crash of 1929, Americans began to realize that they were not living through a mere monetary panic, but that they were entrapped in one of the great crises of their generation. The economic collapse spared few individuals as business activity declined drastically. The gross national product of $87 billion in 1929 shrank to $41 billion four years later. Every day factories closed their doors, and scores of banks and businesses failed. Americans were gripped by a fear of worse things to come. The economic crisis crushed the human spirit, particularly of the growing number of individuals who lost their livelihood. In 1930 the jobless numbered 7 million; by 1931 their ranks had swelled to 12 million; and in 1932 the unemployed totaled 15 million out of a total labor force of 45 million. Rural Americans often were no better off than were their city neighbors. Hundreds of thousands of farmers lost their properties because of foreclosures; those who stayed struggled with the depressed market and found it difficult to earn even subsistence incomes. In some agricultural areas of the Midwest, desperate, angry farmers revolted and formed the National Farm Holiday Association. Led by Milo Reno, they organized boycotts. To achieve higher farm prices they blockaded roads to prevent farm products from reaching city markets.

The Depression created a host of social problems. The loss of a job—and the status that went with it—caused suffering and brought much personal unhappiness into the lives of millions of Americans. Families were disrupted. Some took to the road in a vain search for better employment opportunities elsewhere. Often the women in families sought to earn an income for the first time. Sometimes families moved in with friends or relatives. Other families disintegrated as individual members tried to make it on their own. Many young men and women—perhaps as many as 2 million—became "tramps," riding the rails to nowhere in particular, hoping to get a job or a meal at every stop. Numerous others were homeless—sleeping in parks, subways, or abandoned buildings. Thousands gathered on the outskirts of towns or near river fronts, where they built primitive tar-and-paper shacks. These new communities were called Hoovervilles—ironic monuments to the president who had promised Americans a prosperous New Era. In many communities hungry people could be seen in back alleys, searching garbage cans for scraps of food.

Discontent was expressed through organized protests. Jobless men and women marched through the streets of New York and Chicago to draw attention their plight. Groups of angry farmers with pitchforks and rifles prevented local banks from seizing the property of their neighbors. The Hoover Administration appeared insensitive to the plight of the sufferers. When an organization of World War I veterans called the Bonus Expeditionary Force descended on Washington, D.C., in the summer of 1932 to express their support for congressional legislation that would allow bonus payments for war veterans, President Hoover panicked at the presence of these peaceful protesters and called out the United States Army to disperse them.

The bewilderment of the American people filtered into the political ideology. With the deepening crisis all kinds of nostrums and remedies were proffered by critics of Hoover, who swore that they could set the country on its feet. To Communists the Great Crash signaled the collapse of the capitalist system; to socialists, an opportunity to build a new utopian commonwealth; to neofascists, the dawn of a new totalitarian era; and to a host of less doctrinaire groups, an opportunity to place their special programs before the public. Although the faith of many Americans in the democratic system was shaken, these dissidents made surprisingly little impact upon most voters.

The Great Depression disrupted American foreign policy. Economic crises throughout the world wrought havoc with United States foreign trade, bringing serious dislocations in the nation's exports and imports. And nations that owed war debts and reparations to the Allies found themselves unable to keep up their payments.

Like an epidemic, between 1929 and 1933, economic crisis spread to the industrial nations of Western Europe and Japan. Great Britain reeled under the impact of declining trade and growing unemployment. By 1931 its economy was so fragile that the Bank of England announced abandonment of the gold standard for the British pound. France and Germany were beset by similar problems, including high unemployment and violent fluctuations in their national currencies. The Depression unleashed ripples of discontent throughout Europe and the Far East. Millions of people lost their jobs, their life savings, and their homes. In addition American businessmen found shrinking markets since the Depression was global.

A growing atmosphere of fear, distrust, and insecurity throughout the world also led to the failure of American efforts to secure disarmament. With high hopes President Hoover in 1930 sent a delegation to the London Naval Conference to seek an agreement on naval reduction among the world's leading naval powers. Bitter wrangling between England and Japan and a recalcitrant attitude on the part of the French led to failure. In the atmosphere of distrust, generated in part by the Depression, international disarmament had become an unpopular cause.

By 1931 Americans watched the outbreak of open warfare in the Far East, when Japan launched a military invasion of Manchuria. As one of the more highly industrialized provinces of China, Manchuria was one of the most valuable regions in Asia. The Japanese invasion was a violation of the Open Door Policy of the United States and of the Nine Power Treaty that Japan had signed at the Washington Conference of 1922, and also of the Kellogg-Briand Treaty of 1928, in which Japan had agreed not to resort to war. The Hoover Administration vehemently protested Japanese aggression in Manchuria and the creation of a Japanese puppet state there, but a majority of the American people were unwilling to sanction any use of American military forces to chastise the Japanese or to support effective action by the League of Nations. American protests, therefore, remained largely rhetorical. Secretary of State Henry Stimson proclaimed the Stimson Doctrine, in which the United States declared itself unwilling to recognize any nation, such as Manchukuo, that was established as a result of military aggression. The Manchurian crisis contributed to undermining principles of American diplomacy such as the Open Door Policy and self-determination.

THE GREAT ENGINEER AND THE GREAT DEPRESSION

Great crises in the affairs of nations require great leaders. And in 1929 many Americans felt fortunate to have as distinguished a Chief Executive as Herbert Hoover in the White House. Not only had Hoover served successfully in other important public positions, but he was regarded as a man of vision, a man who had a clear sense of America's future. Throughout the 1920s Hoover's staff had carefully nurtured his public image as The Great Engineer, a man who was equal even to the greatest challenges.

Hoover was a prototype for the self-made man. Born on an Iowa farm in 1874, he was orphaned at the age of ten, whereupon he moved to Oregon to work on an uncle's homestead. After working to put himself through Stanford University, he became a mining engineer. Within a decade he achieved fame and fortune in his field. By World War I he was devoting most of his time to public service and had gained particular prominence as director of the U.S. Food Administration under President Woodrow Wilson. Between 1921 and 1928 while serving as Secretary of Commerce, he dominated the Harding and Coolidge Cabinets. Considered the most prominent Republican of his generation, he won the first elective office of his distinguished career in 1928, the presidency of the United States.

Unlike most politicians, Hoover developed a comprehensive philosophy about national goals and the duties and limitations of government. A lifelong Quaker, his career strengthened his firm belief in individualism as a basic foundation of a democratic society. Individualism, he wrote, resulted in the highest fulfillment of each person's potential. Competition among individuals brought out the best in them and so benefited society as a whole. Hoover was by no means a follower of the nineteenth-century laissez-faire doctrines of Adam Smith. Rather, he looked forward to an associational society, a society in which individuals would form voluntary groups. Such associations would undertake rational, scientific planning to cope with the economic and social problems of a complex technological and industrial society. The role of governments at various levels was to stimulate and encourage these groups, but not to intervene directly to resolve a society's problems. Such intervention, Hoover firmly believed, would undermine individual initiative and the very vitals of democratic government.

The private Herbert Hoover differed considerably from the Hoover fashioned by public relations specialists. According to the public image, The Great Engineer was an original thinker, super organizer, dynamic leader, a man who could solve the big problems that stymied others—be they in mining, engineering, business, social welfare, or government. Unfortunately, the image presented was embellished. Hoover may have been a good organizer, but only in situations where he controlled clear channels of command. Where leadership was dependent on persuasion and compromise, as is so often the case in politics, he was not particularly effective. He tended to be intolerant of critics and unwilling to modify even those ideas or programs that had proven to be unsuccessful. In addition a certain shyness about showing emotion hampered his leadership image during times of crisis.

As a man known for his successful handling of major problems, many Americans believed that Hoover would be adept at dealing with the economic crisis. In the eyes of numerous Americans in 1932, however, the president proved singularly ineffective in coping with the greatest challenge of his long, outstanding career.

Certainly Hoover worked hard to alleviate the Depression. He summoned business and labor leaders to the White House and urged them to avoid panic; he persuaded Congress to create a Federal Farm Board that would purchase farm surpluses as a means of maintaining stable agricultural prices; he created a national committee to solicit voluntary contributions for the unemployed and formed many other committees to deal with social problems; and by 1932 he acquiesced to the establishment of a government bank, the Reconstruction Finance Corporation, whose purpose was to extend loans to ailing businesses and financial institutions. Yet the severity of the Great Depression made many of his efforts futile. Certainly his belief that Americans needed to organize more effectively as a means of confronting the problems of a technological society was inherently sound, but his profound conviction that such associational activity must be voluntary rather than subject to governmental action hampered the scope of his policies. Meanwhile, increasing numbers of Americans were coming to feel that only strong government policies could help the growing chaos and re-create some form of order. Although Hoover was leaning toward greater use of governmental powers by 1932, he refused to abandon his cherished ideals concerning the sanctity of individualism and voluntary cooperation. In 1933 the tired and worn president was possibly the most ridiculed and hated man in the nation, just as in 1928 he had been its most admired public figure.

THE POLITICS OF DESPAIR

Optimistic forecasts by administration officials notwithstanding, the United States' fate in 1932 was perhaps more precarious than at any time since the Civil War. Many Americans wondered whether the democratic system would survive the shattering blows of the Depression. Too many had lost their homes, their livelihoods, and most important, their self-respect. Despite the dispirited mood, the Republicans renominated Herbert Hoover in June 1932.

Active competition for the Democratic presidential nomination ensued between former New York Governor Alfred E. Smith, who had been the party's candidate in 1928, and his erstwhile protege, Franklin D. Roosevelt, the incumbent governor of New York. After a bitter battle Roosevelt was nominated on the fourth ballot. To their surprise the conventioneers learned that their candidate would break precedent by appearing before them in person to accept the nomination. Roosevelt announced, "I pledge you, I pledge myself, to a new deal for the American people." Although he had few specific proposals for combatting the Depression either then or throughout his campaign, he promised vigorous governmental action. Such pledges fell on sympathetic ears, and on election day 23 million cast their votes for Roosevelt as compared to 16 million for Hoover. Roosevelt won the urban minority vote in the large cities of the Northeast and Midwest. He secured substantial segments of the farm vote in the Midwest and the West, in addition to carrying the traditionally Democratic South. The electorate appeared to have given Roosevelt a mandate for change.

But four months lay between the election and the inauguration, and in the interval the Depression relentlessly worsened. The political vacuum that followed the election contributed to the crisis. During these months Hoover and Roosevelt met on various occasions to discuss pressing issues at the White House, but they found few areas of agreement. Roosevelt also listened to suggestions from all quarters, but kept his silence and did not commit himself to any one program or proposal during this period.

Franklin D. Roosevelt was elected to the presidency during one of the worst crises in the nation's history. Millions of Americans were uprooted from their homes, their jobs, and their families. Never before in America had fifteen million people been unemployed. Never before had so many suffered hunger and want, and lived under such wretched conditions as in the decade after 1929. America's future, which had seemed so bright during the 1920s, looked shattered beyond repair in the Hoover era. And the Depression unleashed a vicious cycle of poverty, social unrest, and political turmoil which each year became more intense. Many feared that the Depression would destroy the foundations of American democracy. Certainly Herbert Hoover had shown himself to be incapable of dealing effectively with the disaster. Nor had he been able to retain the confidence of a vast majority of the American electorate. Whether another leader could revive the tottering system was an open question, for some argued that it was beyond repair. It was in this gloomy atmosphere that Franklin D. Roosevelt looked cautiously to the day when he would assume the heavy burdens of the presidency, and the country looked to him with hope.

CHAPTER 2

The New Deal Begins:
The Hundred Days

On March 4, 1933, millions of Americans sat by their radio sets listening to the ceremonies marking the inauguration of the new president. In the nation's capital the weather matched the nation's mood. It was a somber day, cold and gray. A chilling drizzle fell steadily upon the heads of the onlookers and dignitaries, further dampening their spirits. Yet, in this gloomy atmosphere, Franklin D. Roosevelt himself stood out as a symbol of joviality and optimism. After taking the oath of office from Supreme Court Chief Justice Charles Evans Hughes, Roosevelt launched into a memorable and stirring inaugural address. "The only thing we have to fear," he said, "is fear itself, nameless, unreasoning terror."

Roosevelt did not promise easy solutions to the grave problems the nation faced, but he did exude an infectious optimism in his ability and in the ability of the American people to best the crisis. At a time when millions of people in the United States had lost faith in themselves and in their leaders, Roosevelt's call to action had an electrifying impact. Indeed his ability to rejuvenate the American spirit was perhaps more important than any of his particular programs. Still, in the succeeding three months he moved quickly to initiate laws and programs that he hoped would ease the Depression.

AMERICA'S NEW PRESIDENT— FRANKLIN D. ROOSEVELT

Many who had voted for Roosevelt in 1932 really knew little about the man; rather, the voters were registering their rejection of Herbert Hoover and expressing a desire for change. But large numbers of Americans were soon captivated by the new Chief Executive. His picture was hung on the walls of millions of homes. People who had never met him looked to him as a friend. The White House mail swelled to more than 80,000 letters a week, most reflecting the affection and esteem that millions of individuals felt for the president. Americans also developed an insatiable curiosity about Roosevelt, his past life, his family, and his friends.

Born into an upper-class family, Roosevelt was descended from Dutch settlers who came to New York in the seventeenth century. His forebears had made a prominent name for themselves as ship captains and merchants. Roosevelt's father, James, used his inherited wealth for prudent investments that enabled him to live in Victorian comfort on a sprawling estate in Hyde Park, New York, a few miles north of Poughkeepsie. James Roosevelt married Sara Delano in 1880 although he was twenty-six years her senior. Their only child, Franklin Delano, was born in Hyde Park on January 30, 1882. James Roosevelt was a reserved and retiring man, fifty years old when his son was born. Sara Delano was an aggressive and domineering mother who maintained a strong hold on her son throughout his life. Roosevelt grew up at Hyde Park, where he was educated by tutors. Summers he often spent sailing his own boat at the family's vacation home near Campobello, New Brunswick, or traveling in Europe.

But as Roosevelt neared adolescence even his mother recognized the need for more formal schooling. In 1896 she sent him to Groton—an exclusive preparatory school for students from wealthy families. Roosevelt did well at Groton and entered Harvard College in 1900. Although his academic record at Harvard was average, he threw himself into many extracurricular activities, and in his senior year was elected editor of the campus newspaper, the *Harvard Crimson*. Soon after graduation, in 1905, he married a distant relative, Eleanor

Roosevelt, a favorite niece of President Theodore Roosevelt. Unsure of his career plans, Franklin Roosevelt enrolled in Columbia University Law School, where he was a desultory student for two years before he left without taking a degree. But he did pass the New York State Bar Examination and worked in various New York law offices until 1910. By then, somewhat bored, he had decided not to pursue a legal career.

He turned his attention instead to public life and politics. Inspired by Theodore Roosevelt, in 1910 he campaigned for and won a seat in the New York Senate as a Progressive Democrat. As an active supporter of Woodrow Wilson, Roosevelt was rewarded, in 1913, with an Assistant Secretaryship in the Navy Department. For the next seven years he remained in this position while attracting many favorable comments. His popularity was one reason why in 1920 the Democratic Convention nominated him to run as its vice presidential candidate with James M. Cox. In the campaign he made innumerable speeches and made himself better known throughout the nation. His budding political career was cruelly interrupted in 1921, however, when he was stricken with polio and paralyzed below the waist. For three years he was largely immobilized. But at the urging of his wife and close friends, he slowly sought to reenter public life, although he was never again able to walk unaided. In 1928 he was elected governor of New York, where he supervised an energetic state program designed to meet the problems generated by the Depression. As governor he attracted a great deal of favorable nationwide attention, and thus in 1932, he became a prime contender for the presidency.

Roosevelt was not a dreamer, a profound thinker, or an idealist, but rather, he had a sure sense of what seemed practical or possible. As president·he revealed himself to be a masterful politician. In part his political skill could be attributed to his personal charm, which he used as a potent instrument of manipulation. He also had a gift for self-expression that enabled him to communicate with persons in all walks of life. Roosevelt was as good a listener as he was a talker. Although his charming manner often led visitors to assume that he agreed with their views, he usually kept his own counsel and made his own decisions. Frequently, these decisions were a composite of the whole range of advice he had received from others, honed to what he felt was politically feasible. His sense of timing was superb, and often strengthened his almost legendary ability to negotiate compromises. In combination these qualities made him one of the most skillful manipulators of power in the annals of American politics.

FDR'S ADVISORS

A practical-minded politician rather than a theorist, Roosevelt adeptly surrounded himself with advisors who represented divergent views. Throughout much of his public life Roosevelt's closest political friend and his mentor was Louis M. Howe, who had a background in journalism, but who, by World War I, had decided to devote his whole life to furthering Roosevelt's career. With his face scarred in a childhood bicycle accident, Howe preferred to exercise power behind the scenes. Eventually he moved in with the Roosevelts and became a combination political confidant, advisor, manager, and secretary. Howe occupied a unique place in Roosevelt's life and also won the confidence of Eleanor Roosevelt and Sara Delano Roosevelt. During the presidential campaign of 1932, he played an important role in persuading wavering delegates to come into the Roosevelt camp, utilizing political contacts made for Roosevelt in the course of two decades.

In a different category was the group of advisors known as the Brains Trust, whose views Roosevelt began to solicit while he served as governor of New York. Although membership in the Brains Trust between 1930 and 1934 varied with the particular problem under consideration, Roosevelt invited a few key individuals to advise him with some regularity. They included Raymond Moley, Professor of Public Law at Columbia University, who was a firm believer in strong federal action in the business sphere. He was often accompanied on his weekend trips to Albany and later, to Washington, by A. A. Berle, another Columbia law professor, who was an acknowledged authority on corporations. His book *The Modern Corporation and Private Property,* written in 1932, was a sensation. In it he focused attention on the growth of oligopoly in American business and on the separation of ownership and control that had developed in large corporate organizations. Berle often agreed with Moley about the need for greater federal control over business, but he had greater faith in the ability of the business community to police itself. Another regular in the Brains Trust was Rexford Tugwell, also a professor at Columbia University, whose specialty was agriculture. A firm believer in national planning, Tugwell was an unabashed advocate of federal action to deal with most Depression problems. Occasionally, M. L. Wilson, an expert in farm economics, joined discussions about proposed farm legislation.

Serving in still a different capacity was Sam Rosenman, Roosevelt's legal counsel in Albany. Rosenman was adept at transforming recommendations of experts into simple language that appealed to the press and the public. By the time Roosevelt entered the White House, Rosenman had become one of the president's chief speech writers. Still, the Brains Trusters often clashed over their differing philosophies. While Moley looked toward a Hamiltonian collaboration between government and big business, Tugwell espoused a vision of a Jeffersonian agrarian society. Roosevelt found these clashes stimulating. Although the Brains Trust was most important during the campaign of 1932, its influence continued until the summer of 1933.

Collectively, Roosevelt and his advisors drew upon years of experience in the theory and practice of American politics and reform. Roosevelt himself had been greatly influenced by Theodore Roosevelt's doctrine of the New Nationalism, which emphasized the federal government's responsibility to right the wrongs of industrialism. And he had also absorbed elements of Woodrow Wilson's New Freedom, which favored small rather than large business and government, and the desirability of restoring competition. Not only did he accept the need to maintain competition, but he had been profoundly impressed by the World War I mobilization, which revealed how efficient federal centralization could be in time of crisis. At the same time he and many of his advisors had been deeply influenced in their youths by the Progressive Movement, especially the Progressives' concern for the underprivileged and for social justice in America. This common background shaped the outlook of the Brains Trust as it prepared to deal with the impending crisis.

The New Deal was not so much a consistent, carefully planned, comprehensive program as it was a series of practical responses to the various problems arising out of the Depression. Some persons even felt that there were two New Deals—one emphasizing recovery and relief and another focusing on reform. In recent years scholars have questioned such distinctions, noting that they imply greater order and design in Administration policies than New Deal planners intended.

While some reform measures such as the Tennessee Valley Authority (TVA) or the Securities Act were implemented in 1933, Congress also authorized relief programs such as the Works Progress Administration (WPA) in 1935. In short it is difficult to compartmentalize New Deal measures. Nevertheless, it is true that Roosevelt proposed a significant segment of relief and recovery programs in 1933 and 1934, while he clustered many of his reforms in the years from 1935 to 1937. Perhaps the distinction between two New Deals is artificial, yet political observers detected a decided shift of emphasis between 1934 and 1935.

DAYS OF GLOOM AND EXHILARATION

Roosevelt's inauguration on March 4, 1933, coincided with the lowest depths of the Depression. The night before he entered the White House, a majority of the nation's banks closed, some as a result of impending failure, and others, because they feared a run on their deposits. Business activity reached an unprecedented low—one-half of 1929 levels. Farmers found few profitable markets. More than 13 million Americans were unemployed. Voluntary relief agencies had all but broken down. Despair characterized the mood of many Americans.

While Communists talked of revolution, admirers of dictator Benito Mussolini of Italy spoke of the need for fascism. Talk of the need for strong man rule was not unusual in the U.S. press and in private conversations. Americans desired order.

Roosevelt's immediate problem was to avert what many feared might be the impending collapse of the American economic and political system. Roosevelt himself shared this apprehension. His prime aim, he often said, was to save American democracy. He decided on three immediate steps. As a means of restoring the nation's confidence, he officially closed the nation's banks on March 5, 1933, by declaring a "bank holiday." To prevent a drain of specie from the United States, he limited gold exports, basing his authority to do so on an old World War I statute, the Trading with the Enemy Act of 1917. Finally, he called a special session of Congress to convene on Thursday, March 9, 1933, to prepare further emergency measures. Senators Robert M. LaFollette and Edward P. Costigan, two prominent Progressives, visited him the day before the special session, apparently to urge nationalization of the nation's banking system, which he resolutely refused. Like the Hoover administration, he favored maintenance of the existing structure through close cooperation between government and bankers. Unlike Hoover, however, the decisiveness of his actions and his political finesse won him widespread nationwide support.

Roosevelt faced a frightened Congress, which heard his proposals for dealing with the immediate crisis. Few members were inclined to long debate: they listened to the president's message, and they wanted action. In essence Roosevelt advocated government aid to banks so that they could safely reopen their doors. The Emergency Banking Act, which provided for federal loans to distressed banks and created guidelines for reorganization of shaky institutions, was passed. By the evening of March 9, both houses rushed the bill through, and by 9 P.M. Roosevelt had signed it.

During the first week of Roosevelt's presidency, the nation sighed with a sense of relief that now, at last, it had a Chief Executive who did not shrink from the actions needed to restore a semblance of order.

Roosevelt held his first news conference on March 8. He set the tone with an upbeat, friendly, informal atmosphere that won over many members of the press. "It is very good to see you all," the president told the assembled journalists. "My hope is that these conferences are going to be merely enlarged editions of the kind of very delightful family conferences I have been holding in Albany for the last four years." He announced that he would not continue President Hoover's practice of receiving written questions only, and instead, would look forward to answering queries directly. More significantly, on Sunday night, March 12, Roosevelt used the radio to address Americans directly in the first of his famous "fireside chats." In living rooms across the land, perhaps as many as 60 million Americans listened to the president, who said, "I want to talk for a few minutes with the people of the United States about banking. I know that when you understand what we in Washington have been about, I shall continue to have your cooperation, . . . sympathy, and help." Modulating his magnificent radio voice, he explained the nature of the banking crisis in simple, clear language and outlined the measures with which he proposed to meet it. Unlike Hoover, Roosevelt seemed to be taking Americans into his confidence. They responded enthusiastically by lending him their support—and affection. When seven days later, banks were allowed to reopen, Americans deposited more than $1 billion, which they had previously hoarded out of fear of total economic chaos. During its first week the Roosevelt Administration managed to inject a feeling of elation into the nation that resulted in momentum for further action.

THE HUNDRED DAYS

Roosevelt sought to capitalize upon this momentum by keeping the special session of Congress at work until June. During what came to be called the Hundred Days, he proposed a wide range of emergency economic and social legislation that was designed to create order and stability in the nation. Although he did not always get his way as Congress sought to assert its own independence and bridled under the president's spur, nevertheless, this period was a striking display of executive leadership that had few precedents in the American experience.

One of the president's prime concerns was over the nation's depressed agriculture. "Unless something is done for the American farmer," Edward O'Neal, president of the Farm Bureau Federation, told a U.S. Senate Committee in January 1933, "we will have a revolution in the countryside within less than twelve months." Roosevelt instructed Secretary of Agriculture Henry A. Wallace to collaborate with Rexford G. Tugwell, by then Under-Secretary of Agriculture, to formulate emergency farm legislation. Working closely with farm expert M. L. Wilson of Montana State College, and drawing upon more than a decade of experience with farm problems and suggested remedies, they readied what was to become the Agricultural Adjustment Act. The fundamental assumption of this act was that farm production must be limited through balancing of supply and demand to achieve price stability. Since such stability had not been attained through private efforts, government must intervene to create order out of the chaotic price structure that had developed for farm products. One means by which the federal government could persuade farmers to decrease their output was to pay them subsidies for their cooperation. Called the Domestic Allotment Plan, this program met with the approval of the nation's major farm organizations.

The Agricultural Adjustment Act also contained detailed provisions to carry out these objectives. It provided for restrictions on the amount of land to be planted, these to be administered by an Agricultural Adjustment Administration, the organization that was to pay the federal subsidies to cooperating farmers. The cost of the subsidies was to be borne by processors and canners, who became subject to a special processing tax.

A related measure, enacted hurriedly on the same day, was the Emergency Farm Mortgage Act, designed in part to head off a national farm strike threatened for May 13 by Milo Reno, a spokesman for farmers who was dissatisfied with the AAA. This act provided for federal refinancing of farm mortgages by the Farm Credit Administration in the Department of Agriculture. Before the year was out, it had lent $100 million to farmers who otherwise would have lost their mortgages. The Farm Credit Act also consolidated all federal agricultural lending operations in one agency, the Farm Credit Administration.

During the Hundred Days the president and his advisors also tried to bring some order into the chaotic world of business. In his recommendations to Congress, Roosevelt urged them to "provide for the machinery necessary for a great cooperative movement throughout all industry in order to obtain wide reemployment to shorten the working week, to pay a decent wage, . . . to prevent unfair competition and disastrous overproduction." Roosevelt was much impressed by the advice of Raymond Moley and General Hugh S. Johnson, Bernard

Baruch's former associate on the War Industries Board of 1918. These two men felt that the Depression was a result of unrestricted and unregulated competition, which created serious imbalances between production and consumption. What was needed, they reiterated, was suspension of the antitrust laws; they proposed federal supervision of those regulated industries, perhaps even including price control. Stability in industry could only be attained through the creation of a federal agency similar to the War Industries Board, established by Wilson in the First World War, they felt. Some business leaders such as Gerard Swope of General Electric had openly espoused such a remedy as early as 1931.

During April and May 1933 the Brains Trust and its staff worked feverishly to draft legislation designed to reflect Roosevelt's analysis of the crisis in industry. In May Congress enacted the Truth-in-Securities Act, which required corporations issuing new securities to be truthful in their sales brochures or suffer penalties. In 1934 Congress created the Securities and Exchange Commission (SEC) to administer the law. Such legislation had been common on the state level before 1930. Thereafter it had been advocated by President Hoover, but was only passed after a 1933 investigation of the stock market by the Senate Banking and Currency Committee revealed gross abuses by banks and brokers. In addition to the SEC, Congress accepted the president's proposal to establish a Federal Coordinator of Transportation to recommend plans for reorganization of the bankrupt railroads.

The major achievement of the New Deal was the rejuvenation of industry via the National Industrial Recovery Act of 1933. Largely the handiwork of Raymond Moley and General Hugh S. Johnson, the act suspended the antitrust laws for a two-year period and created the National Recovery Administration (NRA), which bore a marked resemblance to the War Industries Board of 1918. Its primary purpose was to try to balance industrial production and consumption. To achieve this goal, the NRA called on more than five hundred major industries or trade associations to draft codes of fair competition. These codes were to govern production quotas, business practices, standards of quality, and methods of competition. Once members of an industry had agreed to a particular code, the NRA and its enforcement agencies sought to secure the widest possible adherence to it. Roosevelt and his advisors had high hopes for this experiment in industrial self-government under federal supervision.

New Deal planners also increased federal supervision over labor. Section 7A of the National Industrial Recovery Act, designed to bolster labor's power and to boost its share of the national income, guaranteed workers the right to collective bargaining and the right to organize unions. It also required NRA codes to provide for minimum wages and maximum hours. To mediate or settle management–labor disputes that might arise over the interpretation of these provisions, Congress created the National Labor Board.

Congress enacted several other measures to bolster economic recovery and feelings of security among Americans. The Glass-Steagall Act of June 16, 1933 contained two important provisions: it required banks to separate commercial banking from investment banking as a means of preventing the stock market speculation that had undermined their stability in the recent past; and the act created the Federal Deposit Insurance Corporation to insure each bank deposit up to $2500. Depositors need no longer fear the loss of their hard-earned savings because of bank failures.

As an avid newspaper reader Roosevelt was keenly conscious of suffering and social unrest caused by the widespread unemployment. He was aware that he must take immediate steps to ease the plight of the jobless. As governor of New York, just a year earlier, he had recruited 10,000 unemployed men to work on forest conservation projects. Roosevelt now saw the possibility of enlarging the New York State experiment to a national scale. On the morning of March 14 he broached the idea of such a work program to Raymond Moley, and a week later, he asked Congress to enact a law to create the Civilian Conservation Corps (CCC). Despite opposition by the American Federation of Labor and some other unions, Congress agreed to the establishment of the CCC on the last day of March. The president announced that the Corps would recruit 250,000 men between the ages of 18 and 25 from families on relief to begin work, he hoped, by early summer.

At the same time Roosevelt listened to the urgings of Harry Hopkins, a social worker from Iowa who had directed relief operations in New York State while Roosevelt was governor. Hopkins advocated immediate direct relief payments by the federal government to unemployed persons to alleviate suffering. "We can eliminate to some extent at least," said the president, "the threat enforced idleness brings to spiritual and moral stability." Direct relief was "not a panacea . . . but . . . an essential step in this emergency." Acting in accordance with Roosevelt's recommendations, on May 12, 1933, Congress appropriated $500 million dollars for relief. The lawmakers authorized the creation of the Federal Emergency Relief Administration to supervise disbursement of the money to state and local governments for distribution. Roosevelt appointed Hopkins Federal Emergency Relief Administrator. Hopkins, however, soon found himself at odds with state and local officials over the quickest and most desirable way of spending these funds. Hopkins was aware, too, that no matter how he distributed the moneys, he could not aid more than 2 or 3 million of the 13 million unemployed.

The president's recognition of the limited nature of relief legislation led him to recommend a more comprehensive public works program. When Congress authorized $3.3 billion for federal public works under the National Industrial Recovery Act, Roosevelt placed administration of the fund in the Public Works Administration under Secretary of the Interior Harold L. Ickes. Although Moley and other Roosevelt advisors saw public works projects as a means of helping business and industry by increasing purchasing power, the president tended to view such projects more as emergency measures than as real stabilizers of the economy.

Meanwhile, Roosevelt could not help but be aware that millions of Americans were in danger of losing their homes as a result of unemployment. Every day during the first half of 1933 foreclosure proceedings forced more than one thousand Americans from their houses. Roosevelt was convinced that the federal government could do something to avert such a disaster. In April 1933, he asked Congress to establish a Home Owners Loan Corporation to buy or refinance mortgages from home owners who could no longer maintain payments. Sometimes the agency advanced money for repairs. At least 20 percent of the nation's home owners availed themselves of this federal assistance, which staved off a total collapse of an already depressed real estate market.

In June 1933 a tired Congress adjourned, thus ending the Hundred Days. The Administration could look back on a spectacular performance, for rarely had a president and Congress worked so quickly to enact so extensive a range of programs. If the New Deal did not restore economic and social order to the nation—an elusive goal—then the policies of these months provided the cement that maintained the fabric of American society.

Looking back just a few months, to many Americans the New Deal seemed to have swept the nation like a whirlwind. No one could yet predict whether Roosevelt and the New Deal would actually lead the country out of the Depression, but millions of Americans were encouraged by what they had observed during the Hundred Days. In contrast to Hoover, Roosevelt had humanized the White House. In a short time he had given millions of Americans the feeling that they had a friend in Washington. And immediate, if temporary benefits from the Administration's legislative programs flowed to businessmen, farmers, and workers. To be sure, the emergency measures did not generate a full-scale economic recovery, nor did they constitute the New Deal's greatest contributions. But Roosevelt perhaps had averted the possible collapse of the American system and had given his fellow Americans a renewed sense of hope.

CHAPTER 3

A Period of Experimentation
1933–1935

Roosevelt had responded to the crisis he found upon taking office with vigorous action. What now remained to be seen was whether that action would be effective. Businessmen, farmers, and workers closely watched the new agencies, while the unemployed looked expectantly to the Administration's relief programs. Whether the New Deal could succeed in lifting the country out of the Depression was a common concern of most Americans during the second half of 1933.

To a considerable extent, Roosevelt's approach to the Depression between 1933 and 1935 was characterized by experimentation. He had no clearly defined program in mind with which to cure the nation's ills. Rather, he preferred to experiment with a variety of alternatives in the expectation that some might succeed—and others might fail. "I have no expectation of making a hit every time I come to bat," he noted. "What I seek is the highest possible batting average," although critics took him to task for this tendency to experiment. As early as May 1932, Roosevelt had said "The country needs, and unless I mistake its temper, the country demands, bold, persistent experimentation."

EXPERIMENTATION IN BUSINESS AND FINANCE

Roosevelt and his advisors looked to the National Recovery Administration as the primary instrument to stimulate business recovery. To head this key agency the president had chosen General Hugh S. Johnson. This feisty army officer had worked with Bernard Baruch in the War Industries Board of 1918 and had gathered extensive business experience in the ensuing decade. A blustering, boisterous and frenetic person, Johnson liked to consider himself a man of action. Within four days after passage of the National Industrial Recovery Act, he had the National Recovery Administration in operation. During the next two months he traveled widely throughout the country to encourage industry representatives to meet with him and with each other to draft suggestions for acceptable NRA codes. His was an almost superhuman challenge, for by early September he had received almost 800 separate codes from industry groups and trade associations.

In part his success was due to a dazzling publicity campaign conducted during the summer of 1933. Johnson employed bands, parades, and speakers to gather support for the NRA. In New York City in early September, more than 250,000 men and women marched down Fifth Avenue to demonstrate their support for the NRA, and similar but smaller parades were organized in towns and cities throughout the land. Meanwhile, General Johnson also conceived of a symbol to indicate compliance with the NRA. The agency's insignia was a blue eagle with spread wings. As President Roosevelt explained, "In war, in the gloom of night attack, soldiers wear a bright badge on their shoulders to be sure that comrades do not fire on comrades. On that principle, those who cooperate in this program must know each other at a glance." General Johnson was more pungent with his comments, saying, "May God have mercy on the man or group of men who attempt to trifle with this bird."

During the next eighteen months, however, the NRA largely failed to achieve its major objectives. The reasons for its shortcomings were complex. Enforcement of codes proved to be one major problem. Since a great many people—in government and out—had serious doubts concerning the constitutionality of the NRA, neither NRA administrators, the Department of Justice nor the courts were prepared to use effective sanctions to secure compliance. By fall of 1933 violations were frequent. At the same time NRA administrators throughout the country found the task of supervising the detailed regulations beyond their bureaucratic competence. Many small entrepreneurs and labor groups feared that suspension of the antitrust laws and collusion by Big Business would lead to a fully cartelized economy. By September 1934 opposition to the NRA was widespread and open, and forced President Roosevelt to request General Johnson's resignation. By 1935 production indices still lagged far behind the levels of 1929, and more than 12 million individuals were still jobless.

General Johnson often felt that much of his frustration with the NRA stemmed from his inability to control public works expenditures and to boost mass purchasing power. That authority the president had delegated to the Public Works Administration headed by Secretary of the Interior Harold Ickes. And Ickes, a miserly, if painfully honest man, personally scrutinized every significant request that came to this agency to make sure that it would not result in fraud. During its first year the PWA disbursed slightly over $100 million. Ickes spent PWA funds so slowly that his agency did not have the hoped for impact in creating new jobs or in generating sufficient purchasing power to spur the national economy.

Meanwhile, the president decided to experiment with the manipulation of monetary policy to accelerate economic recovery. "The United States must take firmly in its own hands the control of the gold value of our dollar," Roosevelt declared, "in order to prevent dollar disturbances from swinging us away from our ultimate goal; namely, the continued recovery of our commodity prices." In particular he toyed with the idea of stimulating inflation in order to raise price levels— thereby generating an increase in industrial activity. The instrument he used was the Chief Executive's authority to manipulate the price of gold, particularly to decrease the amount of gold backing the dollar. Roosevelt moved gradually. In March 1933 Roosevelt, under provisions of the Trading with the Enemy Act, began to move toward the abandonment of the gold standard. In October 1933 he informed the nation that the Reconstruction Finance Corporation would buy newly mined gold at fluctuating prices; and in January 1934 he fixed the value of the dollar at 59.06 percent of its last official gold value when the gold standard was in effect and set the price of gold at $35 an ounce. Unfortunately, the manipulation of the price of gold and devaluation of the dollar did not become the key to economic recovery, as Roosevelt hoped it would.

At the same time inflationists in Congress were organizing their forces, hopeful that an increase in the nation's money supply would generate economic recovery. In April 1933 Senator Burton K. Wheeler of Montana introduced legislation to provide for the coinage of silver at a ratio of sixteen to one—as advocated by William Jennings Bryan in 1896. On the other hand Senator Elmer Thomas of Oklahoma advocated the issuance of greenbacks, or simply, paper money. While Roosevelt was cautious in supporting these measures, he found the political pressures exerted by westerners too strong to resist. In June 1934 Congress enacted the Silver Purchase Act, which instructed the Secretary of Treasury to purchase silver until the supply reached one-fourth of the nation's monetary reserve—or more than $1 billion. Although this measure was undoubtedly of benefit to silver producers in the West, it contributed little to nationwide economic recovery.

The monetary experimentation in which Roosevelt engaged between 1933 and 1935 did not effectively bring the country out of the Depression. As a practical individual, Roosevelt recognized this and began to search for more viable alternatives.

EXPERIMENTATION IN AGRICULTURE

Experimentation also characterized Roosevelt's approach to farm problems between 1933 and 1935. The purpose of the New Deal farm program was clear. Roosevelt hoped to increase the farmers' share of the national income, which had been steadily declining ever since the end of World War I. Such a program required the reduction of output, which would bring an increase in farm prices. The means to accomplish these ends included a reduction of crop acreage, regulation of marketing, a lessening of farm debts, possible general currency inflation (which would benefit debtor farmers), and the expansion of farm export markets. The entire program was to be a cooperative venture between farmers and government. The federal government would act as initiator and guide for the millions of farmers who were to implement programs.

New Deal farm policies were characterized by duplication as well as uncertainty. "I tell you frankly," Roosevelt told Congress, "that it is a new and untrod path, but I tell you with equal frankness that an unprecedented condition calls for the trial of new means." Under Secretary of Agriculture Henry Wallace, Rexford Tugwell, and farm expert G. N. Peek, the AAA moved quickly to reduce the vast agricultural surpluses. Some of its methods, however, invited serious criticism. Faced with increasing overproduction by cotton growers and hog producers in the spring and fall of 1933, Henry Wallace ordered farmers to slaughter 6 million pigs and to plow under 100 million acres of cotton, one-fourth of the 1933 crop. In return the AAA paid producers $100 million. At a time when millions of Americans were hungry and had inadequate clothing, this decision was obviously controversial. In their defense AAA administrators argued that such drastic measures were needed to prevent a total collapse of farm prices. And in October 1933 they organized the Federal Surplus Relief Corporation, which distributed more than 100 million pounds of pork to relief recipients.

Other programs of the AAA were not quite as desperate. Between 1933 and 1935 AAA benefit payments to farmers induced them significantly to reduce their production. The agency also imposed marketing quotas on producers of particular crops if two-thirds voted to impose such restrictions to maintain price levels. Meanwhile, the AAA also tried to expand overseas export markets, as when it boosted Pacific Northwest wheat exports to Japan. Price maintenance was another method used by the AAA. In fall 1933, at Roosevelt's suggestion, it established the Commodity Credit Corporation (CCC). Designed to stabilize production and prices, the CCC made loans to farmers to enable them to keep crops off the market until they could receive profitable prices. AAA efforts to reduce production were substantially aided by severe droughts and dust storms in 1934, which left portions of the Great Plains like deserts. Hundreds of thousands of small farmers and cattle growers were ruined by these catastrophes—and were forced to leave their homes. A substantial number migrated westward in a desperate search for work. This was the worst drought in American experience. One of its effects was drastically reduced farm output. The nation's wheat crop, more than 850 million bushels in 1932, shrank to 550 million bushels in 1935 and led to a rise in wheat prices. Other crop and livestock production declined proportionately.

The curtailment of agricultural output benefited many but not all farmers. The gross income of farmers grew by 50 percent between 1932 and 1936, and farm prices rose by almost 70 percent, but at the same time farmers' total debts decreased by more than $1 billion. The farmers' share of total national income increased from 11 to 15 percent in 1936. Raymond Moley noted that the Agricultural Adjustment Administration was one of the more successful and popular of New Deal programs, and a large number of farmers agreed with that assessment at the time. Without question, however, the AAA tended to benefit medium-sized and large farms more than it did small farmers or southern sharecroppers. Nevertheless, the New Deal restored a semblance of order to the Depression-wracked structure of agriculture. In retrospect it is clear that the New Deal's farm program was based on the belief that farmers should cease to be individualists and instead, seek to solve their problems through cooperative actions.

EXPERIMENTATION IN LABOR

As in agriculture the New Deal's early labor policies were also characterized by considerable trial and error. Since section 7A of the National Industrial Recovery Act was broad and couched in general terms, its real meaning was to be determined by its administrators. Labor leaders such as John L. Lewis, president of the United Mine Workers of America, saw the legislation as a unique opportunity to organize large numbers of workers who were non-union. "The United States Government has said labor must organize," a labor handbill read during an intensive organizing campaign in the summer of 1933. Coal miners, clothing workers in New York, and steel laborers in

Pennsylvania were solicited to join unions. The number of strikes doubled in 1934. Often strikers demanded the right to join a union rather than higher wages. Particularly bitter and bloody were a strike of truck drivers in Minneapolis; a longshoremen's strike in San Francisco led by Harry Bridges, at the time considered an avowed Communist by many; a work stoppage by utility workers in Toledo; and a widespread strike by textile workers in New England and the South. Employers fought back; tensions increased; and by late August 1933 General Johnson had established the National Labor Board in the NRA to deal with labor-management disputes growing out of conflicting interpretations of section 7A. Johnson appointed Senator Robert Wagner of New York as chairman, and three members representing industry and labor were chosen. In its first six months of operation, the board settled thousands of disputes and conducted open elections in which workers were allowed to vote on union membership. But by spring 1934 the board became increasingly impotent because it lacked effective enforcement powers. Employers as well as employees openly flaunted its decisions. Senator Wagner became greatly distressed over the powerlessness of the National Labor Board, and in March 1934 he sponsored legislation to create a new federal labor commission with extensive authority. Since President Roosevelt was still cultivating the support of Big Business for the NRA he refused to give his support to the Wagner Bill.

New Deal labor policies from 1933 to 1935 generated much organizing activity on the part of unions, but they did not create order, nor did they contribute much to decreasing unemployment.

EXPERIMENTATION WITH RELIEF

While Roosevelt was experimenting with programs designed to spur the nation's economic recovery, he was also acutely conscious of the social problems resulting from mass unemployment. In the summer of 1933 many millions of Americans were still hungry, ill-clothed, and homeless or poorly housed. Along with the undercurrrents of bitterness, anger, and frustration were the rumblings of revolution, fanned by Communist agitators and their sympathizers. Relief of social distress could not wait. Yet few of Roosevelt's advisors—neither business nor labor leaders—had constructive plans for dealing with these problems.

Nevertheless Roosevelt was determined to try to do something. Most of the experts who testified early in 1933 before a congressional committee on relief felt that at this point only the federal government had adequate resources for the task.

The agency created to handle relief efforts, with Harry Hopkins at its head, was the Federal Emergency Relief Administration (FERA). Within two days after taking office, Hopkins gathered a skilled staff in Washington and succeeded in creating all the state administrations. The $500 million allotted for distribution to the states was to be matched by the states, who were to administer it by making direct relief payments to the needy. Neither the president nor Hopkins favored direct relief payments, however, except as short-term emergency measures. Both believed that paying men and women to remain idle would undermine their morale, and possibly destroy their sense of dignity and self-respect. Consequently, Hopkins quickly devised a broad range of makeshift work projects for relief recipients. These ranged from street repairs to classroom teaching in bankrupt school systems.

But as the fall of 1933 brought chilly weather, Hopkins brooded about establishing more extensive work-relief programs. Another winter was approaching, and the plight of the unemployed was no better than it had been at the beginning of the year. With the president's approval he created the Civil Works Administration in November 1933, with the avowed goal of employing 4 million people before the year was out. More than one-third of those hired worked on repair of roads and highways. Others helped out in building playgrounds, parks, sewers, and airports. Hopkins never conceived of the Civil Works Administration as more than a temporary expedient, and Congress abolished it in 1934 after it had dispensed more than $1 billion. Despite charges of political corruption and favoritism, the CWA had aided more than 4 million unemployed persons to survive the winter of 1934.

The Civilian Conservation Corps (CCC) was providing work-relief for a limited number of young Americans. By June 1933 the War

Department had made 1,300 camps available. Three hundred thousand men, from every section of the United States, including significant numbers of black Americans as well as American Indians, were enrolled. The Corps engaged in a great variety of conservation projects such as tree planting, forest fire fighting, and forest disease control. The Corps did much to improve national and state parks and beaches, and worked on erosion control projects in thousands of local areas. Within two years the Corps enrolled more than 2.5 million youths who—in addition to receiving a work allowance of $30 monthly—learned new skills or a trade. The CCC was too small-scale to ease the nation's unemployment problem, but it was a popular means of sustaining the morale of a significant portion of America's young unemployed.

To provide financial aid for students and to keep them out of the job market the president in 1935 authorized creation of the National Youth Administration. This agency provided direct monetary stipends for more than half a million college students. Often they performed part-time clerical work for their home institution, whether in libraries or as research aides. One and a half million high school students received similar aid, usually enough to enable them to remain in school. And over two million youths who were not in school also received stipends, often in exchange for work on construction projects. Between 1933 and 1939 the federal government became involved in a wide range of educational activities, prompted largely by the nation's economic crisis.

The New Deal's relief programs, in fact, affected only a segment of the nation's needy. By 1935 approximately 7 million Americans had received some form of federal relief, but 12 to 15 million were still unemployed. Although the New Deal's experiments with social welfare seemed radical to contemporaries, in retrospect they appear to have been too limited to generate economic recovery and full employment. They ameliorated the nation's unemployment problem, but they failed to solve it.

The Administration's record of tentative experimentation from 1933–1935 produced mixed results. The NRA did not prove to be the mighty engine of economic recovery that Roosevelt had hoped it would be. The PWA was disappointing. And monetary manipulation failed to achieve the much desired economic recovery. The Administration's attitude toward labor was so ambivalent that little was accomplished in this sphere. The AAA did succeed in attaining a limited recovery for agriculture.

Despite some successes and some failures, however, the various measures comprising the New Deal during the years of experimentation did not bring economic prosperity and full employment. At best Roosevelt had sustained the hopes of millions of Americans, who sympathized with his efforts to lift the nation out of the Depression—even when they did not succeed. And without doubt the New Deal's economic and social programs during these years cushioned the sufferings inflicted by the Depression on millions of people.

CHAPTER 4

The New Deal Under Attack:
Leaders and Nostrums, 1933–1935

Although the New Deal won a large following in 1933 and 1934, at the same time it aroused vociferous opposition. Convinced Marxists, of course, had never looked upon Roosevelt with much favor, and as he struggled with the Depression they mounted more vehement attacks. They loathed the experimental nature of the New Deal and yearned for a tightly structured government controlled society. At the same time various Neo-Populist critics decried the seeming lack of social conscience on the part of Roosevelt and proffered alternative programs of their own. They were latter-day descendants of Populist reformers of the 1890s, who believed that government should right economic wrongs. Some intellectuals viewed the New Deal skeptically because of its tentative, experimental nature. Economic depression, they believed, required a more thorough reorganization of American society than Roosevelt was prepared to undertake. A very different attitude was expressed by the extreme right of the American political spectrum. Staunch adherents of the status quo, they charged Roosevelt with undermining the very vitals of free enterprise and the American democratic system.

GROWING OPPOSITION TO THE NEW DEAL

The reasons for growing opposition to Roosevelt and the New Deal were varied. Perhaps the most obvious concern of its opponents was the dogged persistence of the Depression. No matter what virtues its defenders might claim, the New Deal failed to bring economic recovery to the nation, nor did Roosevelt succeed in significantly reducing unemployment. At the same time he made many personal enemies. His political decisions often aroused envy and hate. And glaring gaps in the president's legislative programs frustrated many groups. Roosevelt's initial reluctance to undertake extensive social welfare programs, for example, incurred the suspicions of many progressive reformers. Moreover, the passing of the crisis of 1933—when the country had seemed near collapse—vitiated that sense of national unity and purpose from which Roosevelt had benefited during the first Hundred Days. Increasingly, therefore, the anti-Roosevelt forces subjected the New Deal to searching criticism.

THUNDER FROM THE LEFT

The Communist Party of America aimed some of its severest barbs at the New Deal. Expressing a hope that the collapse of the American system was at hand, the Communist Party offered voters its particular programs. In a book published in 1932, *Towards Soviet America,* William Z. Foster, the Communist Party's presidential candidate in 1932, proposed a Marxist program for the reorganization of American society. The experimental nature of Roosevelt's actions to end the Depression was anathema to Foster and other Communists, who felt they already held the key to economic stabilization. They urged the nationalization of all private enterprise in the United States; government ownership and operation of business would create economic order. The abolition of all political parties except the Communist Party would end political strife and establish political order. By embracing communism, Americans would enjoy social benefits denied them by a capitalist system—a living wage, job security, health care, and old age pensions. The Communist program was reiterated again and again during the first two years of the New Deal by Foster and by Earl Browder, a Kansas bookkeeper who came to be the party's leader during the Roosevelt era. Browder said, "The suffering masses have been told to look to Washington for their salvation. . . . But the bitter truth is rapidly being learned that Roosevelt and his New Deal represent the Wall Street bankers and the corporations—finance capital just as Hoover before him." No piecemeal reforms could ameliorate the Depression, the Communists argued. Rather, a comprehensive reorganization of society was needed to bring the nation out of economic crisis. Although the Communist Party had no more than 15,000 members in 1932, its positive program appealed to many more thousands. While most politicians seemed to flounder, the Communists had a clear sense of purpose—and a comprehensive program with which to fight the Depression.

Some Americans were not party members but expressed their sympathy with Communist aims by participating in organizations that were affiliated with the Communist Party. College students were drawn into such groups as the American Youth Congress, the Young Communist League, and the Young People's Socialist League. On most domestic or foreign issues, their spokespersons were sharply critical of the New Deal, and usually espoused the usual Communist positions.

The most distinguished of the Communist fronts during the New Deal was the American Writers Congress, held in 1935. In an ambitious attempt to rally America's leading intellectuals under a Communist banner, the party secured participation of such well-known writers as John Dos Passos, Theodore Dreiser, James T. Farrell, Lewis Mumford, Richard Wright, and Erskine Caldwell. "The capitalist system crumbles so rapidly before our eyes," the Congress declared, "that . . . today hundreds of poets, novelists . . . and . . . writers recognize the necessity of personally helping to accelerate the destruction of capitalism and the establishment of a workers' government . . . Communism must come and must be fought for. . . ." The purpose of the congress was to parade some of America's leading thinkers in a public condemnation of the New Deal. The effort backfired, however, because most of those who participated soon became utterly disillusioned with Communists, particularly as they learned of the extensive Stalinist purges and mass executions occurring in the Soviet Union.

The Socialist Party of America was also attracting a growing following. Led by Norman Thomas, who ran for president five times, the Socialist Party drew nearly 1 million votes in 1932 and made a respectable showing in national, state, and local elections during the thirties. Thomas was an indefatigable speaker. Through the hundreds of speeches he made yearly in the course of his extensive travels, he kept the Socialist position before the American public. He enjoyed cordial personal relations with many leading political figures, including the president and Mrs. Roosevelt. American Socialists drew much inspiration from the Marxist vision of society, but they were more flexible and pragmatic. The Socialists devoted much of their energy to criticism of New Deal measures. In particular they bemoaned Roosevelt's seeming lack of concern for the nation's poor, not only the urban poor but also the sharecroppers and tenant farmers of the South. Thomas focused attention on blacks as well as on whites. Alone among political leaders he stood out as a fervent and articulate advocate of civil rights for black Americans. His stand won him much praise but little political support. "You know, Norman," Roosevelt is reputed to have said to him once, "I'm a damned sight better politician than you are."

NEO-POPULIST CRITICS

Most critics of the New Deal were not as doctrinaire as the Marxist left in the United States. American voters have traditionally spurned ideologues or even reformers who advocate major changes in the structure of the American system. Rather, they tend to support leaders who promise to devote themselves to the solution of specific problems by working within the organizational framework of American society. This, the Neo-Populists did with a vengeance.

The most brilliant of Roosevelt's challengers was Huey Long, the affable United States Senator from Louisiana. Born in the Louisiana backcountry on August 30, 1893, Long received little formal education after he left home as a youth. A fast talker, he rose steadily in state politics. In 1918 he was elected as a state railroad commissioner, after basing his campaign on an appeal to poor backcountry "rednecks." Within a decade he was Louisiana's leading politician. Campaigning on a promise to "make every man a king," Long was elected governor in 1928. During the next four years, he made himself an absolute ruler of the state. He personally directed a vast public works campaign to construct colleges, schools, and roads and bridges; this provided much needed employment. By increasing corporation taxes, he also secured funds to expand and improve public education. Meanwhile, he used the state police to back up his power, occasionally permitting them to manhandle state legislators or coerce political opponents. In 1930 Louisianans readily sent Long to the Senate, which gave him a national platform from which he could—and would—challenge Roosevelt.

Long was unlike any other American politician. Roosevelt feared him as his most powerful political rival and took great pains to cater to him. The senator from Louisiana was a brilliant stump speaker, a vitriolic demagogue who knew how to arouse or to charm his listeners. Although he loved to play his role as the poor man's advocate, Long was equally at home in the boardrooms of corporations. Moreover, the senator was not all bluster. With considerable insight he grasped the need for more comprehensive social welfare policies. Posturing as a Neo-Populist, he advocated a redistribution of wealth in the United States. Long felt the wealthy should underwrite the cost of social programs for the poor.

By 1934 Long was ready to challenge the New Deal and to place his own "Share the Wealth" program before the American public. Although an early supporter of the New Deal, Long was angered by restrictions that Washington officials placed over his right to appoint WPA employees in Louisiana. Moreover, his own personal ambitions to become president were evident. In 1934 he wrote a book entitled *My First Days in the White House,* in which he sketched out in graphic detail what he would do if elected president. Many observers believed that Long planned to run for president as an independent in 1936 and to draw perhaps as many as 4 million votes from the Democrats. Even if he could not prevent a Roosevelt victory in 1936, Long hoped he would attract a significant enough vote to make him a prime contender for the Democratic presidential nomination in 1940.

Long consciously developed his role as a Neo-Populist. With his acute political acumen, he pointed out glaring weaknesses in the New Deal's social welfare policies. Long carefully shaped his own program to fill the vacuum. After unveiling his Share-the-Wealth plan in 1934, Long organized thousands of Share-the-Wealth clubs in every part of the nation to provide him with a grass-roots organization. Long proposed a far-reaching redistribution of wealth in the United States that would provide each American family a home, a car, and a free college education for its children. Affluence for the common people was to be secured via high taxes on corporations and confiscation of private fortunes. Long's plan to end poverty and unemployment in the United States included provisions for free public health programs, vast expansion of public education, extensive public works projects for the unemployed, and pensions for the elderly. His Share-the-Wealth program—fueled mostly by his fiery and brilliant oratory—obviously held wide appeal. Its popularity during 1934 forced Roosevelt to give higher priority to social welfare legislation, if only to forestall Long and his followers. Long's campaign was cut short by his death on September 10, 1935, due to an assassin's bullet. His proposals for social reform, however, did not die with him.

If Long was the most skillful critic of the New Deal, Father Charles E. Coughlin was one of its most consistent detractors. A Catholic priest of Canadian-Irish background, Coughlin had a mellow and melodious speaking voice. As a student at the University of Toronto, he became deeply impressed by the moral wrongs of usury and the need for economic justice in the world. In 1926, while a priest in the Detroit suburb of Royal Oak, Michigan, he began broadcasts of his sermons over Station WJR; soon his "Golden Hour of the Little Flower" attracted thousands of listeners. Every Sunday his soothing voice could be heard attacking bankers, financiers, and Wall Street moguls, pouring venom on men such as Herbert Hoover, J. P. Morgan, and the Rothschilds. Gradually, his sermons took on an increasingly anti-Semitic tone. By 1933 Coughlin was estimated to have a Sunday audience of 10 million Americans, and had become an imposing national figure. During Roosevelt's first year as president, Coughlin supported the New Deal, but when the president abandoned monetary experimentation, he incurred Coughlin's wrath.

In 1934 Coughlin organized the National Union for Social Justice, an organization designed to provide support for his program. That program was not as comprehensive as Huey Long's, but it concentrated on reform of the nation's banking and monetary system. Like the Populists, Coughlin believed that the surest way to end the Depression was through inflation. He was confident that the unlimited coinage of silver and the abandonment of the gold standard were the keys to national prosperity. With increasing rigidity, he viewed these two changes as the only effective means to bring justice to the farmers and workers of America. Coughlin also urged the nationalization of all banks and public utilities in the United States as a means of eliminating what he considered to be the pernicious influence of Wall Street on national affairs. After 1935, when Roosevelt further deemphasized monetary reforms as a cure for the Depression, Coughlin's attacks on the president became more hateful. Coughlin once said, "Is it democracy for the president of this nation to assume power over Congress, to browbeat the Congress and to insist that his 'must' legislation be passed? Is that democracy? I urge you to purge . . . Franklin Double-Crossing Roosevelt."

As Coughlin became more extreme in his anti-Semitism, and in his attacks on the Roosevelt Administration, prominent leaders of the Catholic Church tried to restrain him. After an abortive attempt to enter national politics in 1936, Coughlin's influence waned as Church leaders forced his retirement from public life. His significance in the early years of the New Deal was to carry on the Neo-Populist tradition of cheap money, and to encourage Roosevelt's experimentation with monetary policies.

To most Americans during the Great Depression, the name of Francis Townsend was as familiar as that of Charles E. Coughlin or that of Huey Long. Townsend had an unusual and varied career in his long lifetime. Born in 1867 on an Illinois farm, he spent much of his youth as a farm laborer, miner, teacher, and homesteader. In 1900 he received a medical degree, and for the next twenty years practiced medicine in South Dakota. Soon after World War I he migrated to Long Beach, California, where he sold real estate before he secured a job as a county health officer. In this position he witnessed poverty first-hand, particularly among the elderly. At the time Long Beach had one of the highest concentrations of persons over 65 years of age of any urban area in the nation, about 20 percent. Although by the late 1970s people over 65 constituted about 15 percent of the population, nationwide in 1933 approximately 10 percent had reached this age. And in 1933 in the depths of the Depression, Francis Townsend, at the age of 66, himself lost his livelihood. As he pondered his own fate, and that of men and women in his own age group, Townsend became bitter. And as he grew angrier, he resolved to bring the plight of the aged before the entire nation.

Out of these experiences Townsend developed the Townsend Old Age Revolving Pension Plan. Certainly Townsend's idea did not arise on the spur of the moment, but had grown over a period of years. Townsend said:

> In 1933 when it began to look as if calamity to business would eventually engulf all of us, and we would have to repudiate all obligations of a financial nature and start all over again, the epidemic of despair . . . had reached an all-time high. I had given a great deal of thought to this problem . . . when at the age of 66, I lost my job with the Long Beach health department.
>
> An idea came to me which might alleviate the hopelessness of aged people.
>
> It is estimated that the population of the age of 60 and above in the United States is somewhere between nine and twelve millions. I suggest that the federal government retire all who reach that age on a monthly pension of $200 or more on condition that they spend the money as they get it. This will insure an even distribution throughout the nation . . . thereby assuring a healthy and brisk state of business. Where is the money to come from? . . . A sales tax sufficiently high to insure the pensions at a figure adequate to maintain the business of the country in a healthy condition would be the easiest tax in the world to collect.

Townsend was hardly unique in putting forward a scheme for old-age pensions. Such programs had been widely discussed by social workers, reformers, and politicians for over two decades, but Townsend crystalized much of this debate and captured the imaginations of millions of Americans, young and old. Townsend's plan had several advantages. By requiring compulsory retirement at sixty, Townsend hoped to exclude such persons from the labor market and thus to alleviate some unemployment. At the same time, if the pensioners spent their monthly allowances, they would do much to increase the flow of money in circulation. And, of course, the hardships and sufferings of millions of destitute aged Americans would be relieved through the pension. The cost of such a plan would be high, Townsend admitted, perhaps $2 to $3 billion annually, but it could be met by the imposition of a national sales tax. In this way relief for the elderly would generate economic recovery for the whole nation.

Townsend proved adept in mobilizing widespread support for his proposals. In 1934 he organized the Old Age Revolving Pension Plan, which eventually grew to more than 5,000 local Townsend Clubs. Unemployed teachers or ministers often took the initiative in establishing such community groups. Through speeches, magazines, and lobbying activities in Washington, D.C., and in state capitals, the Townsendites impressed the plight of the aged poor upon the conscience of America. Although Roosevelt and his advisors feared the cost of the Townsend Plan if Congress were to adopt it, they could not ignore him and his followers. In a real sense the provisions for modest, federal old age pensions in the Social Security Act of 1935 were an attempt to still the demands of the Townsendites, although the Social Security Act fell far short of the proposals made by Townsend. Townsend himself considered Social Security unfair and inadequate. Yet it dampened the ardor of many of his followers so that after its passage, the Townsend movement rapidly declined.

Townsend had hoped to broaden the base of his support through collaboration with a group of midwestern, Neo-Populist agrarians led by Congressman William H. Lemke of North Dakota. Lemke was born on a North Dakota farm and early in life came to know the hardships of small farmers on the Plains. After graduating from the University of North Dakota, he attended Yale Law School. Soon he was back in his native state, however, where he became a prominent politician in the Non-Partisan League, the neo-socialist party that dominated North Dakota politics between the two World Wars. In 1932 Lemke was elected to the House of Representatives. There he emerged as one of the champions of the distressed farmers on the Great Plains. Almost two-thirds of the farmers in his own state lost their properties due to foreclosure. Between 1933 and 1936 Lemke sponsored a series of bills to lighten the debt loads of farmers, to postpone foreclosures, to allow refinancing, and to issue greenbacks. Lemke saw himself squarely in the Populist tradition and took pride in his agrarian radicalism. Since the Roosevelt Administration opposed most of his proposals, by 1936 Lemke—once a nominal Republican—openly opposed the Administration.

Lemke led a new party composed of New Deal opponents. In July 1936 Coughlin, Townsend, and Gerald L. K. Smith—a self-proclaimed successor to Huey Long—united in their support of Lemke as presidential candidate of a newly formed Union Party. Although the party claimed to represent 20 to 30 million voters, it consisted of a rather unlikely combination. Except for their hatred of Roosevelt, the party chiefs had little in common. In fact, within a month, rivalries among the leaders largely disrupted whatever influence the Union Party might have had. In the elections of November 1936 the party drew fewer than 1 million votes.

INTELLECTUALS

To many intellectuals, academicians, writers, and thinkers who eschewed Marxism, the Neo-Populist programs of Long, Coughlin, Townsend, and Lemke seemed unsophisticated. In their view only far-reaching changes in the organization of American society could lift the nation out of the Depression. And while Neo-Populist critics of the New Deal had the support of millions, the intellectuals could only count on a following in the tens of thousands. Nevertheless, their views were sometimes important in shaping the attitudes of New Deal administrators responsible for policy formulation.

The American Commonwealth Federation was one of the more significant critics of the New Deal and its programs. Founded in 1932 by

Selden Rodman and Alfred Bingham, two young college graduates with upper-class backgrounds, the federation sought nothing less than the reconstruction of American society. In his book *Insurgent America: The Revolt of the Middle Classes,* Rodman explained his plan of reorganization. Meanwhile Bingham edited the federation's journal, *Common Sense,* which attracted leading intellectuals to its pages. Philosopher John Dewey wrote extensively for it, offering criticisms of New Deal programs and suggesting alternative measures for coping with the Depression.

Less influential than the American Commonwealth Federation were the Technocrats. Founded by Howard Scott, an engineer, and Harold Loeb, a journalist, the Technocrats attempted to analyze the Depression scientifically. A modern industrial society, they believed, could function effectively only with large-scale, comprehensive planning. The absence of such planning had led the nation into the morass of economic crisis. What was needed, therefore, was a drastic change in American values and institutions. Technical efficiency must replace economic profit as a main goal of society; economic planning by specialists and experts must replace democratic processes and institutions. Planning was necessary not only for the economy, but for society as well. The Technocrats envisaged planned communities—in cities, rural areas, and suburbs—to create an orderly, scientifically organized society. Since they couched many of these proposals in obscure language, however, the movement lacked mass appeal. Yet its emphasis on social and economic planning struck a responsive chord among both supporters and critics of the New Deal.

FASCISTS

The Depression policies of the New Deal and the alternatives suggested by its critics in the 1930s developed at the very same time that totalitarian movements were sweeping through Europe. In Russia Communist dictator Joseph Stalin was becoming increasingly repressive; in Germany Adolf Hitler unveiled the Nazi system; in Italy Benito Mussolini instituted a fascist dictatorship; and in Spain Francisco Franco aped his Italian neighbors. Inevitably, then, the followers of these totalitarian movements in the United States sought to further their respective causes. The Communist Party of America faithfully followed the policies determined by its counterpart in the Soviet Union; and a German-American Bund—composed of American Nazis led by Fritz Kuhn—agitated to institute Nazi policies in the United States. At the same time American proponents of fascism advocated their brand of totalitarianism as an alternative to the New Deal. Fascism's leading exponent in the United States was Lawrence Dennis, a Georgian of upperclass background who, after graduation from Harvard, spent a decade in the Foreign Service. After some experience as an investment banker in New York, during the first years of the Depression, Dennis became convinced that capitalism was doomed, and that the efforts of the New Deal to save it were futile. He explained his reasoning in several cogently written books. One, *The Coming American Fascism* (1936), provided a blueprint for a fascist government in the United States. In urging the abolition of the existing American system, Dennis proposed creation of a centralized dictatorship. A fascist state would have absolute control of the economy and could eliminate unemployment, especially by increasing military expenditures. In a fascist America the suppression of all political parties except that of the fascists would result in political stability. And a strident nationalism and aggressive foreign policy would bring national unity to a divided America. With slight improvement in economic conditions after 1933, the fascist movement did not attract a significant following, but it aroused concern and alarm. Novelist Sinclair Lewis became so disturbed about the specter of fascism that he wrote the book *It Can't Happen Here* to warn his fellow Americans of the potential danger.

ECHOES FROM THE RIGHT

Among Roosevelt's most vitriolic detractors was the extreme right. Some of the richest individuals in the nation became increasingly disturbed by the New Deal, opposing most governmental social and economic programs. In 1934 members of the DuPont family—which controlled the nation's largest chemical corporation—organized the American Liberty League specifically to oppose Roosevelt and his programs. The DuPonts provided most of the money used to further the league's lobbying and publicity ventures. Other rich individuals who contributed included bankers such as Winthrop Aldrich. A few of Roosevelt's personal enemies also joined the league, most notably, the embittered Al Smith. The league made little pretense of offering a positive program to combat the Depression; instead, its leaders vented their hatred on the president and castigated the whole range of New Deal legislation. One of their oft-repeated charges was that Roosevelt sought to establish a socialist dictatorship in America.

Some of the criticism Roosevelt got was inevitable for any administration in power—as a seasoned politician such as the president realized. Roosevelt was still acutely sensitive to the most telling charge of his critics, namely, that the New Deal had failed to put the nation back on the road to economic recovery. That much-sought-after goal still seemed distant in 1935. With the presidential election of 1936 looming on the horizon, one of Roosevelt's chief goals was to steal the thunder of his most important critics and to soften their strident demands. Even if he could adopt only a portion of their suggested programs, Roosevelt reasoned, he would still be able to attract large numbers of their followers to his own banner. So he paid some attention to the suggestions of the Socialists for greater government aid to the nation's poorest farmers, to Long's loud cries for social welfare legislation, to Coughlin's urgings for greater monetary inflation, and to Lemke's complaints about the need for additional farm credit legislation. Roosevelt also appeared to be impressed by the call of intellectuals for more emphasis on national planning. In fact, the only groups he totally ignored were totalitarian ideologues and the advocates of rigid laissez-faire, both of which reflected his distaste for extremism. By adopting portions of the proposals made by the various critics of the New Deal, Roosevelt was able to win the support of many of their followers, while at the same time, deflating the importance of their leaders. Thus, in 1935 the president was fashioning a program that was an amalgam drawn from a varied range of proposals made by his opponents. This program was to constitute the nucleus of the New Deal during the next four years.

CHAPTER 5

The New Deal and Reform, 1935–1939

By 1935 various pressures on Roosevelt were leading him to shift his approach to Depression problems. In 1933 he had largely been concerned with economic instability and the possible collapse of the American system; in 1934 he tried experimental legislation to lift the country out of the Depression; but the persistence of the Depression in 1935 seemed to dictate another approach—an emphasis on reform. This was also not an unwise strategy for a politician who had to run for reelection in the coming year. Moreover, in the first half of 1935, the Supreme Court had handed down a series of decisions that all but invalidated the New Deal. Most far-reaching was *Schechter* vs. *U.S.*, in which the court unanimously declared the NRA unconstitutional. Other decisions negated New Deal farm and labor legislation. The Supreme Court's actions were a clear indication to the president's opponents that they could prepare for another round of combat.

THE REFORM PERSUASION

The president's own convictions also played some part in persuading him that the time was ripe for a greater emphasis on reform. Throughout his political career Roosevelt had shown sympathy for reform causes. In 1910 as a freshman state senator in the New York Senate, he had aligned himself with reform Democrats against Tammany Hall, the New York political machine; as a member of the Wilson Administration, he had attracted reform Democrats who supported his vice-presidential nomination in 1920; and between 1928 and 1932, as governor of New York, he developed one of the most reform-minded state administrations to be found anywhere. Thus, it seemed unlikely that Roosevelt would put aside his predilections for reform after he reached the White House. Rather, he suspended them temporarily while he dealt with the immediate pressing problems of the Depression, but once these had been stabilized, the reform instinct in him could be expected to emerge again.

As Roosevelt viewed the nation's problems in 1935, long-range reform might be more effective in dealing with the Depression than the short-range solutions already tried. The crisis seemed too deep-seated, too deeply rooted in structural weaknesses in the American system, to be remedied by palliatives. Nothing less than substantial modifications in the economic and social structure of the nation were required to make the system function more effectively, Roosevelt reasoned. He was not seeking to transform American capitalism, but rather, to preserve and strengthen it by protecting it against its own worst excesses. This could be accomplished by increased federal supervision to ensure the more efficient operation of American institutions. In 1933 Roosevelt had hoped that Big Business could assume prime responsibility for leading the nation back to prosperity. But by 1935 he came to the conclusion that his faith had been misplaced, and that the federal government must assume the role of policeman, or arbiter, among the contending interest groups in American society. He felt it necessary to implement on a national scale many reforms already being administered by local and state governments between 1900 and 1933.

By 1935 former Progressives were urging Roosevelt to take a more pronounced reformist stance. As a sense of crisis abated businessmen had become increasingly disenchanted with the New Deal, and they now openly attacked it. At the annual meeting of the U.S. Chamber of Commerce in May 1935, speaker after speaker arose to condemn Roosevelt and his policies. Meanwhile, at a White House meeting during this same period, Progressive senator Robert M. LaFollette,

Jr., urged him to take the lead in the reform movement. Similar advice came from Professor Felix Frankfurter, of the Harvard Law School. Frankfurter shared many views of Supreme Court Justice Louis Brandeis, who had once been a close advisor of President Woodrow Wilson in formulating the doctrines of the New Freedom. Brandeis advocated smallness rather than bigness, in a decentralized rather than a centralized society. He abhorred Big Business, which he considered to be inefficient economically and dangerous to political democracy. Hoping to restore a more competitive society, Brandeis believed that the federal government could function best as supervisor of orderly and regulated competition. Roosevelt was well acquainted with his views, which were also espoused by Frankfurter and scores of dedicated New Dealers.

Thus began one of the more far-reaching reform movements in the history of American politics. Between 1935 and 1937 Congress, at Roosevelt's prodding, undertook the reorganization of the economic system, the environment, and social policies. Although the pace of reform ebbed after 1937, the reforms also extended to the reorganization of government itself.

REORGANIZING THE ECONOMIC SYSTEM

Amid the continuing Depression, Roosevelt launched a comprehensive program in 1935 to strengthen the structure of the American economy. With the NRA invalidated, Roosevelt now threw his support behind legislation designed to bring greater order into the nation's banking system by expanding federal supervision of it. The Banking Act of 1935 increased the authority of the Federal Reserve Board in various ways. It permitted the board to regulate discount rates to determine reserve requirements of member banks, and to buy and sell in the open markets. The act also authorized the board to issue new types of federal bank notes, thus providing the federal government with more direct control over the nation's monetary system.

The strengthening of federal regulatory authority was also evident in the Holding Company Act of 1935, designed to affect the nation's utility companies. In an effort to create orderly and regulated competition, this act required the integration of utility companies and their subsidiaries—largely in the hope of increasing their efficiency. At the same time section 11a of the act required dissolution of most utility holding companies. Such holding companies had been common in the utility industry since 1920, and in the opinion of many experts, were responsible for much waste, inefficiency, and instability in this segment of industry. In addition the act required all utilities to secure approval from the Securities and Exchange Commission for new securities issues, a provision designed to discourage fraud and inefficiency.

Other legislation was also designed to bring greater stability to the power industry by increased federal control. The Federal Power Act of 1935 created the Federal Power Commission, which was given extensive authority to regulate the rates charged by companies engaged in interstate business. In a supplementary act in 1938, Congress granted the Federal Power Commission the right to regulate the price of natural gas flowing between states. This legislation supplemented one of the New Deal's proudest accomplishments, the Tennessee Valley Authority (TVA), established in 1933 after more than a decade of efforts by Senator George W. Norris of Nebraska. The TVA was a government corporation that operated a multipurpose development in seven states of the Tennessee Valley and engaged in the production of public power, flood control, soil conservation, improvement of river navigation, forest conservation, and development of recreational areas. The development attracted widespread praise. In addition, by competing with private public utilities, the TVA put pressure on them to provide efficient service at low rates and set a "yardstick." Under the leadership of Harcourt Morgan and David Lilienthal, the TVA was a vivid demonstration of the New Deal's determination to create regulated competition via federal controls.

Drawing on the advice of Brandeis, Frankfurter, and Progressives hostile to Big Business, early in 1937 Roosevelt revitalized the Department of Justice's antitrust division. He appointed Yale Law School Professor Thurman Arnold as Assistant Attorney General, and provided him with a large staff to undertake extensive investigations and prosecutions. Within two years Arnold had initiated ninety-two major antitrust actions. Meanwhile, Roosevelt appointed a Temporary National Economic Committee to investigate monopoly power in the nation's major industries. After exhaustive inquiries the committee advocated the dissolution of companies characterized by monopolistic power; however, the advent of World War II prevented the implementation of its recommendations. In fact, the antitrust phase of the New Deal did no more to lift the economy out of Depression than did the NRA, but it represented an effort to increase competition within industry with the hope that such competition would contribute to the revival of prosperity.

Federal supervision of competitive practices in business was also a major goal of the Miller-Tydings Act of 1937. Sometimes known as the Fair Trade Act, it required retailers to sell nationally advertised products at price levels stipulated by manufacturers. This effort to avoid cutthroat competition and price instability was but another attempt to establish a stable price structure that would lessen the economic chaos seemingly created by the absence of federal planning and regulation prior to the New Deal.

Since the Depression had also torn apart the nation's transportation system, the New Deal planners hoped to bring order and stability to the industry by placing it under federal supervision. Roosevelt recoiled from the suggestion that the federal government nationalize the rail carriers, and between 1933 and 1935 Federal Coordinator of Transportation Joseph B. Eastman never did more than to advise carriers on more efficient modes of operation. But by 1935 Roosevelt and his advisors concluded that government supervision of competition would result in a more efficient and balanced transportation system for the nation. The railroads were already operating under the regulatory power of the Interstate Commerce Commission, but other forms of transport were still free from federal controls. Acting in part on Eastman's recommendations, the Administration persuaded Congress to approve three measures: (1) the Motor Carrier Act of 1935, which placed the nation's trucking industry and inland waterways under the authority of the Interstate Commerce Commission, which was granted powers to regulate rates, services, and routes; (2) the Merchant Marine Act, which provided the maritime industry with government subsidies and loans, to be administered by the U.S. Maritime Commission; and (3) the Civil Aeronautics Act of 1938, which established the Civil Aeronautics Board to regulate rates, routes, and services. These three acts effectively reorganized the nation's transportation system.

During its reform phase the New Deal sponsored additional legislation to promote stability in agriculture. One of its more successful measures was the Rural Electrification Act of 1935, which provided low-cost federal loans to farmers who sought access to electric power. In a few short years this act resulted in the electrification of more than 90 percent of the nation's farms.

Meanwhile, bitter disputes broke out between various factions in the Department of Agriculture over extension of more federal aid to the nation's poorest farmers. Many New Deal agricultural programs benefited middle-class or rich farmers, but not the poverty-ridden sharecroppers, tenant farmers, and farm laborers, even though this group constituted one-third of America's farmers. In response to their pleas, and with a hope of conciliating the various factions in American agriculture, Roosevelt threw his support behind the Bankhead–Jones Farm Tenancy Act of 1937. This measure authorized federal loans to tenants to enable them to become self-sufficient land owners, and provided for limited resettlement of farmers currently living on exhausted or nonproductive lands. It also sought to provide aid to the increasing number of farm migratory workers.

One of the New Deal's last significant farm-reform measures was the Agricultural Adjustment Act of 1938. It reiterated many provisions of its predecessor in 1933, but also attempted to meet constitutional objections voiced earlier by the Supreme Court. The Agricultural Adjustment Administration controlled farm production by making soil conservation payments to those who cooperated and by allowing the imposition of marketing quotas if two-thirds of the farmers producing a single crop desired them.

Roosevelt was not particularly anxious to extend federal regulations to the sphere of labor relations, but pressures from organized labor narrowed his options on this issue. Preoccupied with the problems of economic recovery that seemed so elusive, the president was loath to enter upon experiments in social planning unless they would directly contribute to ending the Depression. The National Labor Board, created under the NRA, became increasingly frustrated by its lack of authority, and by 1935 it was virtually impotent. The invalidation of the NRA by the Supreme Court in the *Schechter* decision was the final blow.

During this phase United Mine Workers President John L. Lewis was seeking to spur his reluctant colleagues in the American Federation of Labor to organize workers into industrial rather than craft unions, for the vast numbers of unorganized workers in manufacturing industries were unskilled. Lewis and the advocates of industrial unionism were convinced that without federal support, their organizing drive would have scant success in view of strong opposition from Big Business. In Congress labor's leading spokesman, Senator Robert F. Wagner of New York, was sponsoring a bill to extend benefits labor had enjoyed under the NRA, namely, federal guarantees of the right to organize and bargain collectively. Roosevelt did not actively support the Wagner Bill, although he could scarcely oppose it. Despite the president's reluctance, he had few options but to approve the bill after Congress passed it by a large majority.

The Wagner Act of 1935 was organized labor's Magna Carta. It prohibited a broad range of unfair labor practices by employers—among them the organization of company unions. The act also guaranteed labor the right to organize and bargain collectively. In order to assure the effective administration of these provisions, the act established a new National Labor Relations Board (successor to the National Labor Board created in 1933), appointed by the president. Its functions included hearing complaints by workers or employers and conducting elections where workers sought to organize into unions. The immediate impact of the Wagner Act was to spur unionization and to stimulate the organization of the Congress of Industrial Organizations (CIO), the nation's largest industrial union. In a broader sense the Wagner Act did much to systematize employer-employee relations in the United States. It was an essential building block in the construction of the organizational society.

The Fair Labor Standards Act of 1938 further extended federal guidelines concerning labor management relations. It stipulated minimum wage levels throughout the United States (25 cents an hour) as well as a maximum 44-hour work week. At the same time it embodied the hopes of reformers for more than a half century by prohibiting child labor.

The main thrust of the varied measures that comprised the reform New Deal's economic program was to reorganize the American economic system on a firm foundation. Believing that unrestrained competition and laissez-faire had contributed heavily to the Great Depression, New Deal planners hoped to repair the American system. This could be done, they believed, by letting the federal government play an increasingly important role in maintaining economic stability, in supervising contending economic interests, and in regulating competition.

REORGANIZING THE ENVIRONMENT

The crisis of the Great Depression also spurred New Deal efforts to organize the nation's environmental resources more effectively. From early childhood Roosevelt had felt a deep love for nature. As president this passion did not wane. Soon after he entered the White House, Roosevelt instructed his advisors to work on various phases of conservation programs. "Unlike most of the leading nations of the world," he noted in 1934, "we have so far failed to create a national policy for the development of our land and water resources." The development of such a policy was one of his fervent hopes.

Roosevelt did much to invigorate existing conservation agencies. The activities of the Forest Service were considerably expanded. Roosevelt himself prevailed over skeptical experts to promote the planting of 200 million trees in a one hundred-mile zone along the one-hundredth meridian on the Great Plains. Stretching from Canada to Texas, the shelterbelt was designed to break up winds and to avoid the disastrous dust storms that had swept away surface soils. With the enactment of the Soil Conservation Act (1935), the Soil Conservation Service in the Department of Agriculture took on the task of preventing soil erosion on a national scale. Similarly, the Taylor Grazing Act of 1934 protected the vast cattle ranges of the West by stipulating federal regulations for users of federally owned range lands. To coordinate the increasingly numerous federal programs concerned with the environment, the president on June 20, 1934, created the National Resources Board (after 1935, called the National Resources Committee). The board did much to stimulate local resource planning and encouraged development of regional plans, acting only in an advisory capacity however, since existing organizations such as the departments of the Interior and Agriculture and the Corps of Engineers became increasingly jealous of possible encroachments on their powers. Although the New Deal fostered a variety of specific conservation programs, Roosevelt's desire to formulate a comprehensive national policy concerning the environment thus was not fully realized. Yet the New Deal focused the attention of Americans on the need to develop more systematic resource policies.

REORGANIZING AMERICAN SOCIETY

More than any other single event, the Depression highlighted the unequal distribution of wealth in the United States. Although Roosevelt did not propose profound changes in American society, he did seek a more equitable distribution of economic and political power in the United States by shifting more from the upper to the middle and lower classes.

Roosevelt was keenly aware of the sharp impact of federal taxing powers in separating classes of Americans. Throughout the first half of 1935 the president was clearly on the defensive against the growing popularity of Huey Long and his Share the Wealth platform. Hoping to steal Long's thunder, in 1935 Roosevelt sent a tax message to Congress, influenced in part by Louis Brandeis and Felix Frankfurter, who were urging an attack on concentrated wealth. The president asked Congress to redistribute wealth by new taxes on inheritances, gifts, and high incomes, and by corporate taxes that increased in relation to the size of a corporation. This program aroused bitter reaction from business groups and occasioned a lively debate among the lawmakers. After Congress revised his proposals and enacted the Wealth Tax Act of 1935, the program was much more moderate than Roosevelt's original plan. It increased gift, estate, and capital stock taxes and contained an excess profits levy. Although far less sweeping than Huey Long's proposals, it clearly indicated Roosevelt's determination to use tax powers for limited social planning.

The struggle for a national social security system was just as heated. Demands for social welfare legislation came not only from some of Roosevelt's sharpest critics—Huey Long, Francis Townsend, and Father Charles E. Coughlin—but also from social reformers such as Abraham Epstein, Paul H. Douglas, Harry Hopkins, and others who had been advocating some form of federal welfare programs since the turn of the century. Social Security represented the culmination of decades of agitation and planning, rather than an innovation. Beset on all sides by conflicting demands for various forms of social welfare, Roosevelt reacted with characteristic caution. He appointed a Special Committee on Social Security, chaired by Secretary of Labor Frances Perkins, which represented some but by no means all of the divergent viewpoints. Out of the deliberations of this committee came recommendations that ultimately found their way into the Social Security Act of 1935. Considering the many proposals for federal social programs made at the time, it was really a very moderate and tentative approach by the federal government. On the other hand, it represented a milestone in federal social policies.

The Social Security Act of 1935 reflected the president's effort to reorganize American society by removing fears and insecurities induced by unemployment, illness, or old age, and so to stabilize social tensions. It provided for unemployment insurance, aid to the needy, and old-age pensions. To provide some economic security against joblessness, the act established a fund, administered largely by the states, from contributions by employers and employees. The law also provided for direct federal aid for dependent children, the blind, deaf, or disabled, achieved with matching federal and state funds. In addition an omnibus measure created a pension fund for certain categories of workers over sixty-five years of age, drawn from tax contributions by employers and employees.

The act had some drawbacks in a depressed economy. By requiring employer and employee contributions, the measure had a deflationary effect since it took money out of circulation. Moreover, its coverage of individuals was limited, and no provision was made for joblessness due to extended illness. Still, it was a beginning.

Housing and health also had a place in the social reform proposals. "I see one-third of the nation ill-housed, ill-fed, and ill-clad," Roosevelt noted during his second Inaugural Address in 1937, and he was determined to take effective action to improve conditions for those in greatest need. Congress responded with the Wagner-Steagall Act of 1937, which established the United States Housing Authority. This agency was authorized to grant $1 billion in loans and subsidies to public housing authorities for slum clearance and public housing projects. Roosevelt also sponsored legislation for national health care, but the strong opposition of the American Medical Association helped to defeat the bill in Congress.

Some of the New Deal planners also had visions of a more orderly and content society, to be achieved through governmental planning. Rexford G. Tugwell, in particular, saw a new America, "a land in order, wisely used with the hills green and the streams blue." To achieve this happy society, community planning was essential. Roosevelt, too, felt that new land settlements could provide subsistence homesteads for at least a portion of the unemployed, and that a better balance between city and country life in the United States could be established. This was first attempted in the National Industrial Recovery Act in 1933, under which Secretary of the Interior Ickes created a Subsistence Homestead Division that was designed to attract rural as well as urban slum dwellers to newly planned, self-sufficient demonstration communities. The first project was built in Arthurdale, West Virginia, at considerable cost to the federal government. During the next two years the New Deal sponsored sixty more model communities. Although many of the settlers who came improved their lives, no more than 7,000 individuals were involved in these community experiments. And most of the unemployed were not prepared for life in a cooperative, anyway.

In 1935 Roosevelt consolidated the various rural planning efforts by creating the Resettlement Administration. In addition to resettling farmers from exhausted lands in well-managed, federally sponsored cooperative farm communities, the Resettlement Administration also created Greenbelt towns, model suburban communities that took their name from Greenbelt, near Berwyn, Maryland, a showplace for the program. None of the experiments in community planning attracted widespread support, and by 1937 Roosevelt ordered the liquidation of the programs.

REORGANIZING AMERICAN GOVERNMENT

Roosevelt's vision also embraced the reorganization of American governmental institutions, particularly the judicial and executive branches. Soon after his smashing electoral victory at the polls in 1936, he sent Congress proposals to reorganize the Supreme Court. Throughout 1935 and 1936 the president had been increasingly irritated by the majority of conservative justices on the Court, who had invalidated many of the New Deal's major programs. In 1935 the Court had invalidated the NRA in *Schechter v. U.S.*, the Railroad Retirement Act in *Railroad Board v. Alton Railroad,* and the Farm Mortgage Act in *Louisville Land Bank v. Radford.* In 1936 the Justices declared the Agricultural Adjustment Act unconstitutional in *U.S. v. Butler,* and the Guffey Coal Conservation Act in *Carter v. Carter Coal Co.* In 1937 Roosevelt feared the Wagner Act and the Social Security Act might meet a similar fate. Thus, he advocated the Judicial Reorganization Bill of 1937, which proposed to grant the president authority to appoint a new justice to the Supreme Court, up to a maximum of six, for any justice who did not retire after reaching the age of seventy. Much to Roosevelt's surprise, his Court reorganization plan aroused a storm of fury. He was accused of trying to pack the Court. Many prominent leaders in his own party, such as Senators Carter Glass and Walter George, openly denounced him as a would-be dictator and usurper of judicial power who would eventually undermine the democratic process. The Republicans were even more vehement. So powerful was the combined opposition to the judicial reorganization bill that in July 1937 Roosevelt withdrew it. The battle deeply divided the Democratic Party and eroded some of the president's support. Within two years, ironically, four justices died or retired, and Roosevelt was able to place on the Court men whose thinking was more compatible with his own.

Roosevelt was more successful in reorganizing the executive branch of the federal government. In 1937 he appointed a group of experts in public administration headed by Louis Brownlow to the President's Committee on Administrative Management. Their task was to recommend improvement of the government's vast bureaucracy. Congress adopted some of their recommendations by approving establishment of the Executive Office of the President, which authorized a staff of six administrative assistants to aid the president in his conduct of public business. In addition a number of overlapping federal agencies were consolidated in the interest of administrative efficiency.

THE NEW DEAL AND ORGANIZATIONAL SOCIETY

Administrative reorganization was the last segment of the New Deal's reform program. After 1939 the waging of World War II in Europe created issues that dominated Roosevelt's attention. Then, too, the passions of reformers seemed to have spent themselves in the extraordinary burst of legislative and executive energy that characterized the years between 1935 and 1939.

What the New Deal accomplished during this period was a comprehensive reorganization of American society. Economic reforms modified the structure of the American economy as the federal government—through regulatory and direct action—assumed major responsibility for modulating booms and recessions. New Deal social welfare legislation attempted to stabilize the effects of economic insecurity by having the federal government assume increasing responsibility for problems of old age, unemployment, and housing. And since these expanded public functions greatly increased the size and scope of the federal government—in Washington and throughout the nation—the New Deal's administrative reforms were designed to render the workings of bureaucracy more efficient.

The total effect of much of the New Deal reform program was to accelerate the growth of an organizational society. Such a society depended on the action of groups rather than of individuals. New Deal policies accelerated the organization of interest groups in formal organizations such as business, agriculture, and labor, and these groups, which represented large numbers of individuals, became important influences in shaping federal policies, policies that expanded the role of government in most phases of American life. Roosevelt was one of the founding fathers of the welfare state in the United States, and also one of the progenitors of the organizational society in America.

CHAPTER 6

Minorities in the Great Depression

Among the unheralded reforms of the New Deal was greater recognition of the role of minorities in American life. Until 1933 ethnic and racial groups achieved only limited visibility in politics and public life. This was true of many ethnic Americans who were first- or second-generation descendants of immigrants, particularly the Irish, Italians, Germans, Poles, and Jews. Black Americans, Native-Americans, and Spanish-speaking Americans, eager to play a greater role, were submerged in American society. Constituting almost one-third of the American people, these minority groups looked to the New Deal to help them achieve a more prominent place in American society. If Roosevelt was not exactly the avowed champion of minorities, he still displayed a sympathetic attitude toward their aspirations, thereby earning their overwhelming support.

MINORITIES AND THE NEW DEAL

Since New Deal programs were broad in their appeal, they also embraced some of the desires of minorities. By emphasizing equal rights for all Americans, to be achieved through governmental action, the New Deal attracted millions of minority Americans who came to feel—rightly or wrongly—that they had a sympathetic friend in the White House. And with good reason, for this Administration did not ignore these groups as previous presidents had done. Roosevelt and many of

64

his advisors believed that most forms of ethnic, racial, or religious discrimination emanated from poverty or economic exploitation. Improvement of economic conditions for minorities, they felt, would strike at the roots of prejudice. The sons and daughters of the millions of immigrants who had poured into the United States at the turn of the century, in turn, were particularly fearful that the scant economic and social gains they had made in earlier decades would become casualties of the Great Depression.

Also unlike his Republican predecessors, Roosevelt appointed members of minority groups to public office. From 1920 to 1932 only one of every twenty-five judicial appointees was a Roman Catholic, for example, but from 1932 to 1940 at least one of four were.

Roosevelt's policies about minority groups paid off. Clustered in the great cities of the Northeast and Midwest, minority group persons voted Democratic tickets in overwhelming numbers in 1936 and 1940. Of 106 cities with more than 100,000 population, Roosevelt captured 104 in 1936. Minority groups gained enough power to be instrumental in 1936 in abolishing the Democratic Party rule requiring a two-thirds majority for the presidential nomination, a requirement often used by southern Democrats to exert strong influence.

Many American Roman Catholics gravitated toward the New Deal and the Democratic Party. In the large cities of the nation, Irish-Americans, along with Italian-Americans, flocked to the Roosevelt banner in large numbers. In the Midwest equally large numbers of Slavic-Americans and other ethnic groups with roots in central, eastern, and southern Europe voted for New Deal issues and candidates whom they perceived would best represent their special interests. Most of these ethnic groups still had a vision of America as a land of opportunity. If the Depression had destroyed that vision, Roosevelt at least promised to restore it.

A majority of American Jews also enthusiastically supported Roosevelt and the New Deal. Since many Jews were first-generation Americans, their parents having immigrated to the United States early in the twentieth century, they, too, feared the loss of any gains they had made in recent years. They not only saw Roosevelt as a protector of their existing status, but viewed him as a leader in the struggle to extend the social and economic opportunities of the middle classes, with which most Jews tended to identify. At the same time the

Roosevelt Administration was somewhat sympathetic to the plight of persecuted Jews in Nazi Germany. Over 100,000 entered the United States under existing quota laws between 1933 and 1939. Conscious of the large number of unemployed in the nation, however, Roosevelt, as well as Congress, was reluctant to provide a haven for larger numbers.

BLACK AMERICANS

The New Deal took greater recognition of the aspirations of black Americans than had any previous administrations in the twentieth century. True, Roosevelt did not support all of the demands of the black community, for he was unwilling to antagonize southern Democrats who occupied key positions on congressional committees and could jeopardize his entire reform program. As Roosevelt said, he had to get "legislation for the entire country passed by Congress. If I antagonize the Southerners who dominate Congressional committees through seniority, I'd never be able to get bills passed."

Although historians have argued over the degree of the New Deal's dedication to the cause of racial equality, the fact remains that the overwhelming majority of black Americans, in a major shift in their voting patterns, enthusiastically supported Roosevelt. From Reconstruction until 1928, blacks had traditionally cast more than 80 percent of their ballots for Republicans. But various conditions were undermining that loyalty. The failure of Republicans to respond to the demands of the black community was especially evident during the Hoover Administration. Moreover, blacks increased their political consciousness when they moved from the rural South to the big cities of the East and Midwest. And since blacks were a marginal group in American society, they were particularly hard hit by the Depression. In short, they were ready to shift their political loyalties. In the election of 1932, a majority of black voters supported Hoover and the Republicans. In 1936 and in 1940 black voters turned out strongly for Roosevelt and the Democratic ticket. In the South as well as in the North, thousands of poor blacks affixed a picture of Roosevelt on the walls of their dwellings, for he projected an image of a friend—if not a savior—of the black community. Black Americans were a significant force in the urban coalition that provided Roosevelt with much of his support.

To some extent Roosevelt earned the support of the black community because of 1 is sensitivity to their desires. Early in his Administration he established a "Black Cabinet" to maintain channels of communication with black leaders. The idea was first suggested to him in 1933 by Charles G. Johnson of Fisk University in Atlanta, who urged Roosevelt to be aware of the special needs of blacks during the Depression. Roosevelt asked Harold Ickes to find black civil servants to fill key federal posts and to relay advice back to the White House.

Ickes asked Clark Foreman, a white Atlanta civil rights advocate, to assemble a representative group to constitute a "Black Cabinet." Foreman invited black representatives from various federal agencies to regular meetings. Among the participants was Professor Robert C. Weaver, of North Carolina A & M College, a knowledgeable political scientist who later succeeded Foreman as coordinator of the group. Eugene K. Jones, who was especially well informed about the problems of urban blacks, represented the Urban League. He also advised the Department of Commerce. Robert L. Vann, a lawyer in the Department of Justice, often spoke knowingly of civil rights issues. Henry Hunt, who worked in the Farm Credit Administration, sought to keep the difficulties of southern black tenant farmers before the Administration, often with limited success. William R. Hastie, one of the more distinguished black lawyers in the nation, spoke from his vantage point as an assistant solicitor in the Department of the Interior. Ira De A. Reid, in the Social Security Administration, was an expert on black poverty. Perhaps the most dynamic member of the group was Mary McLeod Bethune, a college president who came to occupy a high position in the National Youth Administration, and who advocated education for blacks as a means of improving their economic situation. Roosevelt listened more intently to the suggestions of the Black Cabinet than he acted on their recommendations, but his Administration was still the first to make an effort to establish regular channels of communication with the black community. And many black voters felt they were represented in the White House as they had not been before.

Many of the New Deal's economic policies did not significantly affect black Americans since most blacks were largely confined to unskilled or menial jobs and most New Deal legislation was aimed at helping the middle class. The NRA did little to improve the economic condition of blacks, very few of whom were independent businessmen. In fact many codes contained clauses that permitted employers to pay lower wages to black than to white employees. During 1933 and 1934 the TVA was accused of following Jim Crow policies in many of its activities. Only under intense pressure from the White House did the TVA directors increase the percentage of their black employees.

That New Deal farm policies seriously neglected southern black tenant farmers was one of the more serious charges leveled against Roosevelt. Norman Thomas, the Socialist leader, was particularly vociferous in criticizing the New Deal on this issue. In fact, AAA programs in the South tended to displace rural black farm workers and tenants and leave them jobless; perhaps 200,000 blacks were forced into this predicament. As white land owners received AAA payments to take land out of production, they discharged their black workers and set sharecroppers adrift. At the same time the aid rendered by the Department of Agriculture to black farmers was limited. Ninety-seven percent of black farmers lived in the South, but only twenty percent owned the land they farmed. The others were at the bottom of the agricultural ladder—wage hands, sharecroppers, and tenant farmers. Their average income was only three-fourths that of whites, ranging from $200 to $300 yearly. Since the AAA programs affected land owners primarily, many black farmers were largely left out of federal farm relief payments, receiving only small sums, nor were most black tenants eligible for long-term loans from the Farm Credit Administration. At best they benefited from short-term production credit. The National Association for the Advancement of Colored People (NAACP) at its 1934 convention noted that "nearly six million Negroes dependent upon agriculture have found no remedy for their intolerable condition."

In the same year blacks and whites joined to form the Southern Tenant Farmers Union. One of its first demands was that rental and parity payments be made directly to tenants and sharecroppers by the federal government instead of being paid to land owners. In part responding to criticism, the Roosevelt Administration sought to develop programs designed specifically to aid black farmers. Between

1936 and 1939 tenants received a larger share of AAA benefit payments. And the Farm Security Administration now made long-term, low-interest loans available to even the poorest farmers. Almost 1 million black and white farmers received loans to rehabilitate the lands they occupied. Experiments with creation of subsistence homesteads in planned communities were more limited. Fourteen hundred black families were living on thirty-two homestead projects, or about one-fourth of its total projects, administered by the Farm Security Administration in 1940. In short, New Deal farm programs were of genuine help to many black farmers, but they fell far short either in altering the structure of Southern agriculture or in making substantial improvements in the condition of Southern black tenant farmers and farm workers.

The New Deal's relief and social welfare laws did aid many blacks, since they constituted an especially high percentage of the nation's poor and unemployed. Thus, although blacks comprised 10 percent of the nation's population, they filled 18 percent of the WPA rolls. On the other hand, local authorities in the South often practiced discrimination against blacks. In Atlanta during 1935, WPA payments to blacks were significantly lower than those paid to whites. Similarly, southern officials largely excluded blacks from the Civilian Conservation Corps. Only under pressure from Harry Hopkins did the CCC gradually accept blacks equal to ten percent of its enrollment, and, even then, blacks were usually assigned to segregated quarters.

Although the Roosevelt Administration made few deliberate efforts to diminish racial intolerance in the United States, it did set a tone that led to greater integration. Secretary of the Interior Harold Ickes was a particularly vehement opponent of race discrimination, having once served as president of the Chicago chapter of the NAACP. Ickes not only desegregated all cafeterias at Interior Department headquarters in Washington, D.C., but at his insistence the PWA reserved one-half of its housing projects in the South for blacks. All construction contracts awarded by the PWA required the hiring of black workers; this set a precedent for other federal agencies.

First Lady Eleanor Roosevelt also actively supported the NAACP in public and conspicuously appeared at interracial social functions. She was instrumental in arranging a concert by black contralto Marian Anderson at the Lincoln Memorial in Washington during

1939 after the Daughters of the American Revolution had withdrawn permission for Anderson's use of Constitution Hall because of her race.

Still, the president refused to publicly support federal antilynching bills pending in Congress between 1933 and 1939. Ever conscious of the power of southern Congressmen in his own party, he refrained from antagonizing them too openly. Although sympathetic to antilynching legislation, he declined to make it a major issue. In 1938 a group of southerners filibustered an antilynching bill to death in the Senate. Although encouragement from the White House might have cleared the path for the legislation, Roosevelt preferred to remain silent.

The limitations of black influence on public affairs in the 1930s were partly due to conflicts within the black community itself. The majority of blacks were poor and uneducated as well as politically unorganized and weak.

The inability of black Americans to exert greater influence on the New Deal was due to a lack of organization. Blacks constituted neither a strong political nor an economic interest group. In these years they lacked the internal unity, leadership, or skill with which to attain a degree of racial solidarity. As the prominent black leader A. Philip Randolph aptly declared at the time: "True liberation can be acquired and maintained only when the Negro people possess power; and power is the product and flower of organization—organization of the masses, the masses in the mills and mines, on the farms, in the factories." The Congress of Industrial Organizations (CIO) in 1937 was beginning to organize those laboring masses—black and white—but the benefits for blacks would not be visible until the post-World War II period.

Serious internal conflict in the NAACP lessened its impact. The executive secretary of the NAACP during the New Deal was Walter White, an urbane individual who believed strongly in integration through use of the courts and through active public relations. His leadership was sharply challenged by Dr. William E. B. Du Bois, a shy and thoughtful scholar who believed in militant black nationalism and self-help rather than black reliance on the white community. Du Bois felt that White was unsuited to provide leadership for the black masses. Du Bois' resignation in 1934 as editor of *The Crisis*, the organization's mouthpiece, and from the NAACP a year later, seriously weakened the association's influence within and without.

NATIVE-AMERICANS

As one of the more disadvantaged groups in American society, Native-Americans also looked to the New Deal for help and guidance. The annual income of families rarely exceeded $100; their infant mortality was the highest of any group in the United States and the adult life span was the shortest; the education of Indians—fewer than five years on the average—was the lowest of any one racial group in the nation. Indians were plunged into additional misery by the Depression. Moreover, until 1933 federal Indian policies were designed to integrate Native-Americans, even though they resisted this policy and thought it destructive to their own culture.

Although Roosevelt had little first-hand knowledge of Native-Americans and their conditions, he was sympathetic to their special problems. Moreover, Roosevelt placed great trust in Harold Ickes, Secretary of the Interior, who had been intensely interested in the impact of national policies on Native-Americans for many decades. Before being offered a Cabinet post, Ickes had hoped for an appointment as Commissioner of the Bureau of Indian Affairs. As head of Interior, he turned to John S. Collier, a close friend who had long been a champion of Native-American causes. Collier, born in Atlanta, Georgia, spent much of his early life as a social worker. Soon after World War I he became involved with Native-American problems and served as executive secretary of the American Indian Defense Association, a group concerned with gaining more rights for Native-Americans. In addition he edited *American Indian Life,* an important journal dedicated to the discussion of issues relating to Native-Americans. During the 1920s Collier became convinced that the federal government's integration policies had failed. He believed that Native-Americans needed autonomy and self-determination to survive successfully. During Collier's tenure as Commissioner of the Bureau of Indian Affairs (1933–1945), his policy was to encourage cultural pluralism and cultural nationalism among Native-Americans wherever practicable. To be sure, announcing such a declared goal was easier than carrying it out. Nevertheless, policy under the New Deal for Native-Americans was designed to encourage greater self-reliance.

Collier had ambitious plans to make Native-Americans economically independent. He hoped to secure additional lands for many of the tribes through grants from federal and state governments, through court actions, and via private efforts. Such additional lands, he felt, would provide a firm economic foundation that would improve their agricultural self-sufficiency. Among the Navajos, for example, he attempted to improve soil conservation by discouraging overgrazing by cattle, but since the Navajos felt the ownership of stock was a status symbol, this policy clashed with their cultural values.

In an effort to encourage Native-Americans to engage in business ventures on the reservations, Collier fostered the organization of credit unions and provided federal funds for local self-help ventures. Under his direction the Bureau of Indian Affairs encouraged tribes to make credit available to individuals or groups interested in forming businesses. At the same time the bureau placed greater emphasis on hiring Native-Americans for its own staff. More than one fourth of its 5,235 employees during the New Deal were Native-Americans.

Collier experienced only limited success. The problem of unemployment remained serious throughout the Depression. Of the many New Deal agencies in operation the Civilian Conservation Corps particularly appealed to young Native-Americans; many of its conservation projects were well suited to their interests and skills. More than 80,000 youths participated in CCC work in fifteen western states, where their income provided a welcome supplement to their needy families on the reservation. Even so, unemployment among Native-Americans was three times the national average.

In another effort to make Native-Americans self-sufficient and independent, the bureau encouraged tribes to establish formal councils or some formal hierarchy of officials to administer policies on a local level. Since these kinds of formal as opposed to more informal political institutions were alien to some cultures, these efforts were not always successful. Nevertheless, the New Deal era saw the establishment of formal tribal councils and a greater emphasis on self-government than in previous years.

Under Collier the bureau also made a concerted effort to encourage Native-Americans' cultural awareness and independence. In contrast to the policy of previous administrations, which had sought to extirpate Native-American culture in order to hasten integration, the Roosevelt Administration sought to stimulate cultural pride. Since Collier appreciated native religion, art, languages, and traditions and ceremonials, he hoped to preserve them without interference by the federal government or by mainstream society. Under him the bureau's policies were designed to achieve these ends. Tribes were urged to celebrate their own traditions and festivals; artists were encouraged to work in their native style and to display their work; and Native-Americans were encouraged to speak in their native languages.

Collier also attempted to reverse the previous policy of separating children from their parents by sending them away to boarding schools. Spending their teen-aged years away from the reservation weakened family ties and lessened their interest in their own culture. The bureau began to build day schools on reservations so that these youngsters could secure the education they needed to cope with mainstream American society while also being exposed to their own culture in their parents' homes. Since Native-Americans were themselves sharply divided over the merits and disadvantages of integration, Collier's educational plans were not always popular.

The Bureau of Indian Affairs actively supported various congressional measures designed to institutionalize Collier's approach to federal management of Indian affairs. The Johnson-O'Malley Act (1934) created the bureaucratic machinery to provide for closer cooperation between federal and state officials engaged in the administration of Indian policies. This act also clarified the nature of civil rights for this group. More controversial was the Wheeler-Howard Act (1934), which granted extensive rights of self-government to various tribes while diminishing the authority of private traders and missionaries, as well as the Bureau of Indian Affairs and state and local governments. Some large tribes, such as the Navajos, rejected the measure because of their hostility to the federal livestock reduction program. Although limited in its application, the Wheeler-Howard Act helped to crystallize self-sufficiency as one component of federal policy.

SPANISH-SPEAKING AMERICANS

Spanish-speaking Americans were not as self-conscious a group in the 1930s as they were to become several decades later. Their problems were similar to those of other minorities—poverty, a high rate of joblessness, and feelings of political impotency. To a considerable extent the majority of Spanish-speaking voters supported Roosevelt in the belief that they benefited from the New Deal. Since many Hispanic Americans had little earning power, they looked favorably on New Deal social welfare policies. In Texas, New Mexico, and California, they constituted a significant number of workers in the Civilian Conservation Corps, the Federal Emergency Relief Administration, and the Works Progress Administration. Like other poor Americans, they welcomed Social Security. Although Hispanic-Americans traditionally had voted for Republican candidates before 1930, they now came into Democratic Party ranks in large numbers. To some extent, after 1934 particularly, this was due to the political shrewdness of Dennis Chavez of New Mexico, the only U.S. senator of Hispanic background. President Roosevelt frequently turned to Chavez as a spokesman for the Hispanic community. Chavez showed himself to be aggressive as well as skillful in funneling relief and other federal funds into areas with significant Hispanic populations.

The Mexican population of the U.S. increased greatly during the Depression; perhaps as many as one million Mexicans moved to the United States, seeking escape from rural poverty in Mexico, poverty that was far more wretched than that in the United States. Although many of these immigrants—a large portion of whom entered illegally—remained in the Southwest, significant numbers migrated to Kansas, Illinois, and Michigan. Uneducated and unskilled, many became migrant farm workers. Often they labored for wages lower than those demanded by native-born American workers, thus incurring hostility and prejudice. In the Midwest they worked in meat packing plants and on railroad gangs, while in Pennsylvania they joined the ranks of unskilled steel workers. Many of the barrios in American cities were founded—or greatly expanded—by the stream of Mexican immigrants who came during the Great Depression. Local governments such as Los Angeles County, as well as federal authorities, annually deported tens of thousands who had entered as illegal aliens. Called "wetbacks," these were temporary migratory field workers who came to help with the harvesting of vast crops in California and Texas, but did not always return home as their alien status required.

A small trickle of Puerto Ricans came to New York City and a few other large American cities during the Depression. In retrospect they were the advance guard of a large Puerto Rican migration to the United States just after World War II. Seeking escape from the poverty of their native land, they also found few opportunities in Depression-ridden America. Lacking special skills, education, or facility in the English language, many found that they only had escaped from one cycle of poverty to another. Their coming added still another ethnic group to the Spanish-speaking peoples of the United States.

WOMEN

As with other minority groups, during the Depression women discovered that attitudes toward them did not undergo great striking changes. Yet the economic crisis did stimulate a greater awareness among women—as among other minorities—of the forms of discrimination to which they were subjected. The seeds of a more assertive women's rights movement were clearly germinating in the New Deal era. And fortunately, two outstanding women affiliated with the Roosevelt Administration—First Lady Eleanor Roosevelt and Secretary of Labor Frances Perkins—were present to lead the battle.

A minority in terms of oppression if not in numbers, women were subject to great exploitation during the Great Depression as, for example, when Congress singled out women for special treatment in the Economy Act (1933), which reduced federal expenditures for public services. By allowing only one spouse to work on the Federal payroll, the act effectively laid off federally employed wives whose husbands were earning higher civil service salaries. As national policy, this reflected a practice that was widespread in industry. These and other discriminatory practices were vigorously denounced by Eleanor Roosevelt and Frances Perkins. Their protests influenced some New Deal administrators, particularly Hugh Johnson, Administrator of the National Recovery Administration, who championed the inclusion of equal minimum wage scales for men and women in the NRA codes. Despite his efforts, though, about 120 of the approximately 500 NRA codes in operation contained minimum wage levels that did discriminate against women. Such discrimination led to an active campaign by feminist leaders organized within the National Woman's Party. Although it had a small membership it publicized the need for an Equal Rights Amendment throughout the New Deal era.

Eleanor Roosevelt and Frances Perkins attempted to use their influence when possible to secure a larger role for women in the Roosevelt Administration. They also prevailed upon the Federal Emergency Relief Administration to create seventeen camps for women in eleven states. In 1936 the National Youth Administration, for which Mary McLeod Bethune served as an assistant administrator, opened similar facilities. Another project to aid women was also provided by the Works Progress Administration when President Roosevelt appointed Mrs. E. S. Woodward as an assistant administrator responsible for supervising work projects oriented toward women.

The New Deal's record on minorities was mixed. As was reflective of Roosevelt's political style, the New Deal offered minorities less than they desired but more than had been done by previous administrations. The New Deal was a shrewd combination of the theoretically desirable and the politically feasible.

From an organizational perspective, minority groups were encouraged to organize more effectively under the New Deal in order to influence the political process. Minority group members occupied a fair number of important government positions. Black Americans, more conscious of their political power, channeled their demands more effectively through the Black Cabinet. Native-Americans were encouraged in their strivings for greater self-determination in the hope that as a group, rather than as individuals, they could exercise more influence in shaping their own destinies. Hispanic-Americans were similarly encouraged to use political representation to represent their own special interests. And women raised their consciousness to think of themselves as a group. The New Deal gave an impetus to the efforts of minorities to participate more fully in the mainstream of American life by encouraging self-awareness and the forming of interest-group organizations that could influence public policies.

CHAPTER 7

American Culture in the Great Depression, 1933–1939

The Depression shook the values of many Americans, who looked deeper into themselves in the search for an explanation. What had gone wrong? Was democracy possibly not the all-encompassing panacea it had appeared to be? Not surprisingly, some American intellectuals rejected many of their political traditions and briefly flirted with Marxism. Others criticized the system without rejecting the fundamental tenets of American democracy. For the masses, though, the search for an American identity also produced a nationalistic mood, a positive reaffirmation of American values even if the Depression revealed serious shortcomings. These attitudes and values were reflected in the work of writers, musicians, and entertainers of the era.

AMERICAN WRITERS AND THE DEPRESSION

American writers during the Thirties lacked the dazzle of their predecessors in the preceding decade. They also wrote fewer outstanding novels, plays, or poetry and poured much energy into literary criticism. Nonfiction flowered, particularly those forms that explained or attempted to explain what had happened.

If the Depression resulted in reduced sales of books, the trend toward mass marketing continued. The Book-of-the-Month Club was organized in 1936 to stimulate large-scale distribution of hard-cover volumes. At the same time, cost-conscious publishers were beginning to develop a new paperback format for books originally appearing in hard covers. Paperback books, an economy during the Depression, did not become significant until after the Second World War, however.

The quality of many novels appearing during the Great Depression was mostly undistinguished. Various writers of Marxist persuasion made a vigorous if not very successful effort to create a genuinely proletarian literature. They hoped it would serve as a prelude to the revolutionary class struggle, which, they were sure, was imminent in the United States. Thus, novels were used to arouse the revolutionary consciousness of the masses. Many works dealt with class conflict and capitalist exploitation of workers and the poor. Meyer Levin in *The Old Bunch,* Michael Gold in *Jews Without Money* and Grace Lumpkin in *To Make My Bread* and *A Sign for Cain* examined these themes. Unfortunately, the structure of their plots was so poorly conceived and their style so turgid, that these novels—designed, ironically, to appeal to the masses—attracted few readers. Some of the architects of the would-be American proletarian novel received such adverse criticism that they abandoned their efforts. On the other hand, established writers who embraced a Marxist orientation had greater success. The nation's leading black writer, Richard Wright, condemned racism in American society in his profoundly moving *Native Son.* Erskine Caldwell bitingly depicted Southern rural poverty and the system that produced it in *God's Little Acre.* James T. Farrell, using Chicago as a setting in his popular *Studs Lonigan* series, told the story of a young man's degeneration during the Great Depression and described how the capitalist system had spawned it. John Dos Passos wrote the trilogy *U.S.A.* as a Marxist condemnation of American society. Although these works attracted attention from literary critics and from the reading public, they were hardly literary masterpieces, and they did little to raise the political consciousness of Americans or serve as instruments of class struggle.

Other novelists were sharply critical of American life without paying tribute to another ideology. *Butterfield 8* and *Appointment in*

Samarra by John O'Hara were bitingly realistic. As might be expected from a former newspaperman and reporter, O'Hara was a stark chronicler of facts, particularly of the disruptive and destructive influence of the economic crisis upon the values, attitudes, and behavior of the middle class in American society. Similarly, James M. Cain in *The Postman Always Rings Twice* recorded the terror and fear inspired by this decade of crisis. In *You Can't Go Home Again* Thomas Wolfe mirrored the bewilderment of his generation in the face of the collapse of the more secure and settled world of their youth.

Unquestionably the single American novel that best recorded the mood of the American people in the throes of the Great Depression was John Steinbeck's *The Grapes of Wrath*. Like most works that define a generation, this book could not be classified as belonging to any particular literary genre. Steinbeck was a realistic and critical observer of the American scene, but he also endowed his characters with a romanticism that made them representative of the values and feelings shared by millions. In this fictional account of the Joads, a migrant farm family fleeing the Dust Bowl of Oklahoma for the fertile fields of California, Steinbeck recorded the hopes and the dreams, as well as the tribulations and sufferings, of countless Americans during the Great Depression. Although beset with defeat, the Joads never abandoned their humanity nor their hopes for a better future—and this, in a way, epitomized the contemporary American spirit.

Historical romance, as one might expect, provided an obvious avenue of escape during the Depression. The single most popular book of the decade was Margaret Mitchell's *Gone With the Wind,* a novel of epic proportions that chronicled the lives of uprooted southerners during the Civil War and Reconstruction. The parallel was too much for most Americans to resist, and helps to explain its enormous popularity.

The major poets in the United States during the 1930s rallied to the defense of American society by celebrating the values that characterized its past development. Carl Sandburg fortified his reputation as America's troubadour with "The People, Yes," a reaffirmation of democratic ideals. With similar eloquence Archibald MacLeish in the poem "Panic" captured American courage and optimism during the Depression. Stephen Vincent Benet and Edna St. Vincent Millay looked deep into the American past to provide inspiration for their own generation. The message transmitted by these poets was that Americans could take pride in the vision and the stamina of their forebears that could sustain their hopes in their own time of troubles.

The critics used the Depression to pierce what they considered to be the bourgeois veneer of American writing. Granville Hicks in the book *The Great Tradition* and V. F. Calverton in the work *The Liberation of American Literature* discussed America's literary past as a reflection of capitalism and its false values. To them literature was a reflection of politics. Marxist media such as *The New Masses* and *The Daily Worker* reiterated these themes with tiresome repetition. Other critics rejected the association of values with literature altogether. These were the so-called New Critics such as John C. Ransom, R. P. Blackmur, Allen Tate, and Kenneth Burke, who revolted against mass society and democracy. The New Critics explained that literature was the product of an intellectual elite that had the technical skill to divorce form and content. Between these divergent poles were critics who wrote of the history of American literature as a reflection of the humane democratic values that constituted the foundations of American democracy. Van Wyck Brooks, in the book *The Flowering of New England,* took this view. History and biography were especially popular during the Depression. As Americans became aware of other crises in their past and how they were dealt with, they could put the Depression in better historical perspective. Widely read historians included James Truslow Adams, who wrote about the Puritans in *The Epic of America,* and Charles A. Beard, who wrote *The Idea of National Interest,* which explored the origins of American foreign policy. Ralph H. Gabriel in *The Course of American Democratic Thought* explored the origins and development of democratic ideas in America.

Interest in biography reflected the intense desire of many Americans to draw inspiration and guidance from great men and women of the past. Carl Van Doren's book *Benjamin Franklin* enjoyed enormous popularity as did Marquis James' books about Andrew Jackson. One of the widely acclaimed masterpieces of the decade was the four-volume study of Abraham Lincoln written by Carl Sandburg. Former journalist Douglas S. Freeman wrote an equally moving biography of

Robert E. Lee. Allan Nevins published numerous impressive biographies, including *Grover Cleveland: A Study in Courage.*

Popular books about economics and sociology were read with great interest during the New Deal era. One of the writers who sought to explain contemporary technological and economic changes was journalist Stuart Chase, who in his book *Men and Machines,* pleaded for a more centralized and rational economic system. Marxist-oriented writers such as Lewis Corey, author of *The Decline of American Capitalism,* documented what they perceived to be the collapse of the American economy. On the other hand Thurman Arnold, a law professor at Yale, in *The Folklore of Capitalism* enlightened Americans about the great differences that existed between the myths and the realities of their economic system.

During the Great Depression American writers consciously used their craft to comment on the crisis and its impact. Only the Marxist left viewed literature as a weapon in the ideological struggle that they were waging against American democracy. The social critics and romanticists also reflected the influence of economic crisis. Indeed, the impact of the Depression on American culture was as penetrating as on the economy.

THE THEATER IN ECONOMIC CRISIS

The Depression had a devastating effect upon theater in America. As audiences dwindled many theaters were forced to close, bringing large-scale unemployment to thousands whose livelihood was in some way linked to the performing arts. On Broadway in 1932 two-thirds of the New York theater houses went into bankruptcy, and more than three fourths of all the plays closed because so few could afford to attend. Among those to survive was George Gershwin's satirical musical, *Of Thee I Sing,* which lampooned national politics, especially the presidency. Clifford Odets, a talented leftist playwright, wrote *Waiting for Lefty,* a critique of contemporary American society and its economic values. Other leading dramatists of the decade included Lillian Hellman, whose best-known play was *The Little Foxes;* Robert Sherwood, author of *Idiot's Delight,* who appealed to Americans with pacifist or isolationist leanings because of his sardonic indictment of war; and Maxwell Anderson, who wrote *Both Your Houses,* an attempt to dramatize the conflict between realism and idealism among New Dealers.

One unforeseen result of the Depression was its stimulation of amateur theater; more than one thousand local amateur theater groups sprang up during the 1930s.

The American musical play continued to enjoy popularity in this period. George Gershwin composed *Porgy and Bess* (1935), and *Shall We Dance?* (1937), while Richard Rodgers and Lorenz Hart set Americans singing to melodies from *Babes in Arms* (1937), *The Boys from Syracuse* (1938), and *Pal Joey* (1940). Some of the more lilting songs of the decade came from the pen of that urban sophisticate, Cole Porter, whose haunting melodies made musicals such as *Red, Hot, and Blue* (1936), *Leave It To Me* (1938), and *DuBarry Was a Lady* (1939) great successes.

DEPRESSION ART

Like writers, American artists were sufficiently moved by the experiences of the Depression to reflect it in their works. Artists whose work dealt with social protest included William Gropper, a Marxist sympathizer who painted angry satires of capitalism and the individuals who represented it. His painting titled *The Senate* sought to convey his feelings about the hypocrisy, corruption, and selfishness he thought existed in government. His views were shared by another struggling young artist of this era named Jack Levine, whose distaste with the American system was evident in many of his canvases. In *Feast of Pure Reason,* and *The Syndicate,* his hatred of capitalists was conveyed with startling savagery. His style was in keeping with other artists such as Peter Bloom and George Grosz. Among the best known of the social protesters was Ben Shahn, who satirized American politics and his view of its hollowness in such works as *Huey Long, Crowd Listening,* and *East Side Soap Box.*

Another group concerned with the portrayal of American society was the romantic realists. Edward Hopper, one of the more popular painters of this genre, keenly reflected the loneliness and alienation experienced by millions of urban dwellers. *Room in Brooklyn* was characteristic of his paintings on these themes, and *Cold Storage Plant* conveyed his feelings about how humans were dwarfed by industrialization. *New York Movie House* caught a mood of loneliness in a crowded city. If Hopper documented the growth of the urban scene, Charles Burchfield concerned himself with the decline of rural America in such paintings as *Old Farm House, November Evening,* and *Edge of Town.*

Regionalists were considerably more optimistic in their approach to American life, as they celebrated the positive virtues of the American past. Thomas Hart Benton was one of the more prolific in this group. Colorful rather than profound, his works such as *Arts of the West, Cotton Pickers, Country Dance,* or *Cradling Wheat* were vignettes of Americana. Grant Wood brought a highly precise style to his art, reflected in *Churning* or *Parson Weems' Fable.* John S. Curry captured the grandeur of the American landscape in paintings such as *Spring Showers, Sunrise,* and *Corn.* The regionalists used images from the American past to quiet the doubts their contemporaries expressed about the present.

The impact of the Depression on American culture was to stimulate a reexamination of the values which formed it. Writers, dramatists, and artists probed positive as well as negative characteristics of life in the United States. In the process, Americans came to know themselves better than before, and to discover aspects of their heritage of which they had not been aware in previous years.

MUSIC DURING THE DEPRESSION

Although the Depression muted innovation in American music the decade witnessed increasing maturity in the music world. As in literature and art, the economic crisis spurred a surge of nationalistic feelings as well as regional pride among musicians. Dubbed the American

Wave, it reflected a revitalized concern by composers regarding their relation to society. Musicians, as well as other performers, found that the recently developed mass media—radio, recordings, and motion pictures—provided them with vast new audiences in their own country, where they once had to rely on the more appreciative Europeans.

A musical trend toward regionalism and a celebration of historical traditions was reflected in such works as Aaron Copland's tone poem *El Salon Mexico* (1936), which drew upon the traditions of the Southwest. This was true also of his popular ballet *Billy the Kid* (1938), and his musical scores for such films as *Of Mice and Men* (1939) and *Our Town* (1940) also utilized regional themes. Other American composers were inspired by the nation's past. Ross Lee Finney was influenced by colonial hymns, while William Schuman used children's calls (rhymes) for his *American Festival Overture*. A profound appreciation of American folk traditions was also expressed by Virgil Thompson, Roy Harris, and Marc Blitzstein. Thompson's opera, *Four Saints in Three Acts,* written in collaboration with Gertrude Stein, enjoyed an enthusiastic reception from the critics. Harris's overture *When Johnny Comes Marching Home Again* (1934) was a reaffirmation of traditional American patriotism. His *Folksong Symphony* (1940) skillfully wove popular American tunes into a full orchestral work. Douglas Moore, a composer and professor of music at Columbia University, received acclaim for his folk opera *The Devil and Daniel Webster* (1939), which reflected a preoccupation with America's past. At the Eastman School of Music in Rochester, Howard Hanson experimented with American themes in symphonic orchestrations.

American music was greatly enriched by many talented refugees who fled Nazi oppression. Some of the world's greatest composers immigrated to the United States, including Igor Stravinski, Arnold Schönberg, Paul Hindemith, Béla Bartók, Kurt Weill, and Darius Milhaud. They introduced a cosmopolitan sophistication into American music that it had lacked before, and they broke down some of the cultural isolation which had long characterized the American musical scene and did much to make the United States a new leader in the international world of music.

Major symphony orchestras such as the Philadelphia Orchestra under Leopold Stokowski and Eugene Ormandy, the New York Philharmonic under Arturo Toscanini (to 1936) or the Chicago Symphony under Frederick Stock achieved worldwide recognition. In 1937 Toscanini built his own orchestra, the NBC Symphony, into a first-class ensemble whose Saturday afternoon broadcasts took fine symphonic music into millions of homes. Such talented singers as Rosa Ponselle, Lawrence Tibbett, Gladys Swarthout, or Rise Stevens were on the roster of the Metropolitan Opera House in New York City, which had previously relied mainly on European talent.

Popular music in the 1930s took on a lighter tone than was found in the brash jazz of the preceding decade. Americans sought music made for dancing rather than contemplative listening. The jazz of the 1920s gave way to the more easygoing Swing of the 1930s. Most likely the term "swing" derived from Duke Ellington's 1932 recording called *It Don't Mean a Thing If It Ain't Got That Swing.* Small jazz combos were replaced in popularity by the Big Bands. By 1935 Benny Goodman had established himself as The King of Swing, and was rivaled in popularity by Glenn Miller, Tommy Dorsey, Artie Shaw, and Harry James. At the same time "sweet" music bands such as those of Guy Lombardo and Wayne King attracted a wide following as did that soothing crooner Bing Crosby, the decade's most popular singing star. These entertainers enjoyed an unprecedented popularity, since national broadcasting brought them audiences numbering in the tens of millions.

THE GROWTH OF FILM

Hollywood continued its growth as the movie capital of the world. If the 1920s were the golden age of the silent film, the 1930s saw the spectacular rise of sound movies. Films were *the* great escape; each week more than 60 million Americans went to the movies. Some persons went to forget their problems and the grim reality of their Depression-dominated lives; others went simply to escape winter weather. Once inside a movie theater, the average patron entered a world that was very different from the reality of Depression-racked America.

Hollywood, as anthropologist Hortense Powdermaker noted, was America's dream factory. Spectacular musicals such as *No, No, Nanette* and *Broadway Melody of 1936* carried their audiences into an elegant, sophisticated dream world where all was well. Fred Astaire and Ginger Rogers danced their way into the hearts of millions through films such as *Flying Down to Rio, Top Hat, Roberta,* and *Shall We Dance?* Judy Garland became one of Hollywood's brightest stars in her memorable role as Dorothy in *The Wizard of Oz.* Situation comedies such as *It Happened One Night,* with Clark Gable and Claudette Colbert, or *Mr. Smith Goes to Washington,* starring James Stewart, provided pleasant entertainment. Actresses like Lucille Ball, Jean Arthur, Rosalind Russell, and Katharine Hepburn appeared in many of these light-hearted films. Historical romances also enjoyed great vogue. The greatest success in this genre was undoubtedly *Gone With the Wind,* starring Clark Gable and Vivien Leigh—it broke all existing records. Swashbuckling sagas such as *Robin Hood* made actors such as Erroll Flynn national heroes. Gangster movies starring James Cagney, Humphrey Bogart, George Raft, or Edward G. Robinson provided another escape from the routine of daily life during the Depression.

Whatever the genre, films provided an easy escape from daily cares for many Americans, and the world created by Hollywood contrasted starkly with the real America of the 1930s. According to Hollywood, the "good guys" always won, and "bad guys" always lost; individuals who were poor ultimately became rich; virtue triumphed over evil, and the just were inevitably rewarded. How could this fail to appeal to Americans at this time?

THE NEW DEAL AND CULTURAL LIFE

Those who contributed to American culture in the Depression decade suffered as much—or more—from unemployment as did others. Work opportunities for writers, artists, actors, musicians, and teachers were extremely limited in the 1930s. President Roosevelt early became aware of their dilemma. Under the influence of Harry Hopkins, he approved special programs in the Works Progress Administration to provide temporary employment for those in some way engaged in the arts. The result was significant federal support for cultural activities, including the Federal Writers Project, the Federal Theater Project, the Federal Dance Project, the Federal Music Project and the Federal Art Project.

The Federal Writers Project was an ambitious enterprise designed to provide work relief for struggling writers. To organize a highly individualistic group of people such as writers in cooperative projects was no easy task, and Henry Alsberg, the director of the Writers Project, experienced many anxious moments. During the half-dozen years that it was in operation, the project produced almost one thousand publications. Most notable, perhaps, were the fifty-one state and territorial guidebooks, written by teams of writers working under a state director. The guidebooks combined history, folklore, anthropology, geography, and other aspects of the life in a particular state or region. Initially, the projects had been designed to provide temporary relief; they met, however, with great success and enabled many Americans to discover themselves and their local or national heritage. In addition to guidebooks for the states, the writers prepared publications for cities. They also wrote one hundred and fifty books for a Life in America series that included such titles as *The Italians of New York* and *The Hopi.*

The WPA also engaged in the collection and classification of long-neglected historical records. These included Spanish land-grant archives in New Mexico and Arizona, as well as shipping records from colonial New England, and municipal archives in colonial New York. Although a few well known writers such as Conrad Aiken worked on the project, most of its staff was young and not well known at the time. Some, such as John Cheever and Richard Wright, achieved fame in later years.

Considered daring in its day, the Federal Theater Project provided employment not only for needy actors but for directors, set designers, costume designers, and stage hands as well. Harry Hopkins chose Hallie Flanagan of Vassar College, a classmate of his at Grinnell College, to direct the project. She proved to be highly innovative and managed to present hundreds of productions each year without charge to the public; included were circuses, vaudeville, musical comedy, classics, dance theater, and drama. Blacks, who previously had been largely excluded from the legitimate stage, were welcomed. An all-black company performed Shakespeare's *Macbeth,* for example, under WPA sponsorship. It was estimated that more than thirty million Americans attended one or another of these federally sponsored theater attractions.

Unemployed musicians also found the WPA Music Project a haven. In large cities as well as in small towns, the WPA organized community orchestras to perform everything from symphonic music, opera, and chamber music to popular pieces. Los Angeles—where the number of unemployed musicians was especially high—had at least six symphony orchestras in 1937. In some communities WPA musicians offered free music lessons to interested persons. The project encouraged young composers such as William Schuman and provided hearings and critiques that aided their development as artists. The activities of the Music Project were diverse, and also included collecting and cataloguing local American music. In the South and in Appalachia, in particular, previously unrecorded songs were collected and preserved.

Former museum director Holger Cahill supervised the Federal Arts Project, which provided relief to thousands of artists and sculptors. A few of the participants, such as Jackson Pollock, Willem de Kooning, or Stuart Davis, won fame in later years. In hundreds of communities WPA artists taught painting, crafts, sculpture, clay modeling, and carving. Others painted murals in public buildings, many of which still exist today. Despite varying levels of quality, all the murals reflect a rather vigorous native American tradition.

The WPA also provided temporary relief for teachers. Particularly in California the WPA offered adult education classes and pioneered with various types of vocational training programs. It sponsored correspondence and home study courses and special classes for workers' education. Unemployed teachers on the WPA roster staffed new nursery schools that cared for children of low-income families. Dieticians also used their special talents under the WPA. Researchers were put to work for the cause of historic preservation; restoration was done on California missions, Civil War battlefields in the South, and colonial forts in New England and New York.

As the most encompassing event in the lives of most Americans during the 1930s, the Depression was bound to have a lasting effect on American culture. The net result of cultural activities stimulated by the Depression and the New Deal was to heighten the consciousness of the American people about their heritage. Millions of Americans first became conscious of local folklore, regional art and music, past traditions, and democratic values through cultural activities that were a direct product of the commonly shared experiences generated by the economic crisis. The Depression also hastened the formal organization of cultural activities. The New Deal heightened the consciousness of writers, artists, and musicians as groups and, as in the WPA, provided a place for them in the broader framework of national policies. Moreover, the New Deal stimulated the organization of voluntary groups engaged in cultural activities. In this sense the New Deal organized popular culture and gave it a more prominent place in the structure of American life.

CHAPTER 8

The Search for Order in Foreign Policy, 1933–1939

While Roosevelt struggled with domestic issues throughout his first two terms, foreign affairs took an increasingly greater portion of his time and energy in his later terms. During this period Americans were watching the collapse of the European order and the fall of democratic governments throughout the world.

THE DEPRESSION AND FOREIGN POLICY

Understandably, the Great Depression itself created many diplomatic problems for Americans. Instability in the international economy contributed to the depressed economic conditions within the United States and to mass unemployment. The precipitous decline of American exports overseas cost thousands of jobs in the United States. Violent fluctuations in foreign currencies affected U.S. gold reserves and disrupted import and export trade. Withdrawal of foreign investments in 1929 and 1930 added to panic selling and the collapse of securities markets. The impact of the Depression, however, was not solely economic. A troubled economy worldwide led to the collapse of democratic governments in Europe and the rise of militarism, rearmament, and territorial expansion. These actions challenged Americans on two fronts. On the one hand they viewed the rise of dictatorships as a threat to American democratic values. On the other hand, disillusionment over American participation in World War I was widespread, and pacifist sentiment—particularly among young people—was strong. The seeming failure of President Wilson's plans for a stable world order left many Americans embittered and disappointed. They felt passionately that the United States should not immerse itself in the treacherous currents of world politics too deeply.

Isolation thus became the keynote of United States foreign policy during Roosevelt's first term in the White House. In recent years historians such as William Appleman Williams who leaned toward a New Left view have argued that even in the Depression era, Americans were more involved in world affairs than they realized. Such involvement is relative, however. In comparison to Cold War diplomacy between 1945 and 1970, Roosevelt's policies in the 1930s appear to reflect the nation's desire for nonintervention. His policy was to steer clear of European and Asian embroilments while consolidating American influence in the Western Hemisphere. In Congress the desire to retreat into isolation was perhaps even stronger. Meanwhile, various antiwar organizations such as the Veterans of Future Wars and the Fellowship of Reconciliation sprang up and gained strength.

Soon after assuming the presidency, Roosevelt was forced to make a decision concerning American cooperation with other nations in respect to international tariff policies and currency stabilization. Months before he left office, the internationally minded Herbert Hoover had indicated American willingness to work with the British and French to solve the economic problems related to the Depression. In spring 1933 the major European industrial nations were planning a conference in London for June, at which their representatives were expected to work out detailed programs to help the world economy. Roosevelt was beset with conflicting advice concerning American involvement in the London Economic Conference. On the one hand Secretary of State Cordell Hull, long an advocate of free trade, urged him to lower tariff and other trade barriers. On the other hand, though, Brains Truster Raymond Moley insisted that Roosevelt would jeopardize many of his domestic economic recovery measures if he made new international commitments. The choice seemed to be between a nationalist or an internationalist approach to economic recovery. Faced with this difficult choice, Roosevelt wavered. He sent Hull to head the official American delegation at the conference, but on July 3, soon after Hull arrived in London, Roosevelt sent his "Bombshell" message to the conference, in which he declared his opposition to American participation in international efforts to regulate currencies or trade. Hull was stunned, but abided by the decision. Roosevelt's message effectively wrecked the conference and further efforts to conclude international economic agreements in 1933. Without the cooperation of the United States, such attempts were futile.

To some extent the impression of many Europeans that the United States was retreating into greater isolation was mitigated by American recognition of the Soviet Union in November 1933. Disturbed by Japan's invasion of Manchuria, Roosevelt cast a more benevolent eye on the U.S.S.R. as a potential ally. Despite considerable criticism at home, the president extended official United States recognition to the Soviet Union, and in return, the Communist government promised to pay war debts owed to Americans and to abate its propaganda in the United States, two promises it did not keep.

ISOLATIONIST SENTIMENTS GROW

During 1934 American isolationist sentiment was whipped into virtual hysteria by the investigations of the Nye Committee. Established by Congress to explore the causes of American entry into World War I, the committee, which was headed by isolationist Senator Gerald P. Nye of North Dakota, focused its attention on munitions manufacturers. Operating under the assumption that wars were caused by economic forces, the committee charged that the United States had been tricked into World War I by munitions makers. Although the evidence Nye and his staff collected hardly warranted such a conclusion, the committee's work had an enormous impact on the American public and stiffened isolationist resolve.

Partly because of the work of the Nye Committee, Congress responded aggressively to preclude further American involvement in European affairs. In 1935 it approved the Pittman Resolution, which prohibited exports of American arms to war-torn areas. The resolution also prohibited American merchant vessels from carrying munitions into such areas and withheld protection from Americans who travelled on ships belonging to belligerents. In 1936 and 1937 Congress enacted additional neutrality acts to strengthen its resolve of noninvolvement. The Neutrality Act of 1936 prohibited loans to belligerent parties; the act of 1937 forbade arms sales to belligerents and contained a cash-and-carry clause whereby only belligerents who could pay for and transport nonmilitary goods would be permitted to make such purchases in the United States. Unfortunately, the impact of these acts was not what Congress had hoped. They benefited aggressor nations by increasing the difficulty with which those attacked could secure necessary arms. In a sense the legislation only delayed the day of reckoning when Americans had to decide whether or not to join other democratic nations in opposing totalitarian expansion.

For the immediate time, however, the isolationist mood of Americans was also revealed in Roosevelt's diplomacy in the Far East. After more than a decade of discussion, Congress agreed to grant the Philippine Islands, ceded to the United States by Spain after the Spanish-American War, their independence. American sugar producers in particular strongly favored such a move since Philippine sugar competed with their own product. And as long as the Philippines were part of the United States, American tariff duties did not apply. The Tydings-McDuffie Act of 1934 provided for Philippine independence after a ten-year period of transition.

The disinclination of Americans to become too closely involved with European affairs was also reflected in the Administration's refugee policies. As the Nazis stepped up their persecution of Jews and other minorities, a steady trickle of German Jews sought refuge in countries around the world. Although many beseeched the United States to allow them entry, Congress refused to modify the existing quota, which allowed only 150,000 immigrants to enter the country each year. President Roosevelt was sympathetic to their plight but hesitant to take overt action. Furthermore, some State Department workers, such as Assistant Secretary Breckinridge Long, had anti-Semitic leanings. As a result, while about 120,000 German-Jewish refugees were permitted to enter the United States between 1933 and 1941, millions more found the doors closed and eventually perished in Nazi death camps.

Meanwhile, the continued Japanese invasion of China posed real problems for the United States. In 1935 the Japanese armies occupied the five northern provinces of China—in direct violation of the Open Door agreements, the Nine-Power Pact of 1922, and the Kellogg-Briand Pact of 1928. Like Hoover, Roosevelt felt constrained to watch helplessly. His own absorption in the problems of domestic depression as well as the strong prevailing mood of isolation severely limited his alternatives.

On July 7, 1937, the Japanese intensified and broadened their invasion, and in the midst of a full-scale military attack against China, Japanese war planes sank the American gunboat *Panay* off Shanghai. Even in the face of this action, the majority of Americans were still opposed to any overt action by their government. A Gallup poll reported that more than 70 percent of Americans opposed any intervention. And more than a two-thirds majority in Congress voted against imposing any sanctions against the Japanese. In fact, most Americans breathed easier when they learned that the Japanese government had apologized and offered to pay damages for the *Panay*.

Paradoxically, though, the desire to remain aloof from the problems of Europe and Asia led the United States to seek more collaboration with other countries in the Western Hemisphere. With his talent for appropriate phrases, Roosevelt called this new idea the Good Neighbor policy. American concern for national security and solidarity against communism was obviously one motivation, but another was the desire to expand foreign markets during the Depression years. To fulfill this policy, Roosevelt took on the role of diplomat as he sought to dampen strong anti-American feelings throughout South America that were in part a product of United States interventionist policies in the decade following the Spanish-American War.

Like so many of Roosevelt's programs, the Good Neighbor policy embraced a many-sided approach. Economic cooperation was one facet. Congressional action on tariffs was another facet. By 1934 Congress approved the Reciprocal Trade Agreements Act, which allowed the president to negotiate treaties to reduce American tariffs for nations that made reciprocal reductions in return. Within two years Roosevelt had concluded thirteen such agreements, many with South America. During the same period United States exports rose more than 14 percent. The Reciprocal Trade Agreements Act proved to be one of the more successful of the New Deal's foreign policies. Also in 1934 the United States established the Export-Import Bank, which made loans to South American countries seeking to stabilize their currencies.

At the same time Roosevelt took special care to impress Latin Americans with the desire of the United States not to intervene in their affairs. At the Inter-American Conference at Montevideo, Uruguay, in 1933, the United States supported a declaration pledging nonintervention among the Western Hemisphere states. The president underscored this policy by supporting the abrogation of the Platt Amendment, which had given the United States the right to intervene in the affairs of Cuba. In a treaty with Panama in 1936, American negotiators gave up similar privileges. The president withdrew Marines from Haiti in 1934 and joined with representatives of twenty other governments in South America to ratify a Protocol of Non-Intervention at the Inter-American Conference in Buenos Aires, Argentina, in 1936. Roosevelt's personal appearance at this meeting underscored the importance he attached to fostering close ties and goodwill with Latin American countries.

To embellish its image as the friendly giant in the north, the United States also played a positive role as mediator of conflicts in Latin America as, for example, when American officials played a role in settling strife between Peru and Colombia in 1933. Roosevelt assiduously refrained from intervening in the Cuban revolution of 1933, and used great self-restraint in refusing to intervene when Mexico expropriated American oil companies during the 1930s. When Germany and Japan concluded the Anti-Comintern Pact in 1936, nations of the Western Hemisphere adopted the Convention for Collective Security. This provided for mutual consultation in case of attack and brought the United States closer to its neighboring nations than it had been in many years.

THE GATHERING WAR CLOUDS

By 1937, however, Roosevelt began to doubt the effectiveness of American diplomacy in limiting Axis expansion. In 1936 Adolf Hitler marched his troops into the Rhineland, which had been declared a buffer zone at Versailles. In 1938 he occupied the Czech Sudetenland, and marched into Austria as well.

Two years earlier, Hitler's Axis partner, Benito Mussolini, had conquered Ethiopia. In Spain both Hitler and Mussolini provided active military support for their would-be fellow dictator, General Francisco Franco, who was fighting a civil war to overthrow the elected republican government. Fascist politicians were also influential in Hungary and Rumania.

Due mostly to the worsening international situation Roosevelt's second administration saw increasingly heated debate between noninterventionists and interventionists concerning the course of American foreign policy. A strong isolationist policy prevailed. If the president himself had doubts about isolationism, he was careful to keep them to himself. He proceeded with characteristic caution, seemingly anxious not to alienate public opinion, but between 1937 and 1940 Roosevelt took an increasingly firm stand against German and Japanese expansion in Europe and the Far East respectively.

This departure from nonintervention was first heralded in what became known as Roosevelt's Quarantine Address, given in Chicago on October 5, 1937. Prompted by the recently accelerated Japanese advance into China, Roosevelt called for the quarantining of aggressor nations by the international community. Possibly he was sounding out public opinion to determine whether or not isolationist sentiment was weakening, but certainly the tone of the address—and the fiery manner in which he delivered it—was firmer than any of his previous presidential foreign policy statements:

> The political situation in the world, which of late has been growing progressively worse, is such as to cause grave concern and anxiety to all the peoples and nations who wish to live in peace and amity with their neighbors. . . . the peace, the freedom, the security of 90 percent of the population of the world is being jeopardized by the remaining 10 percent who are threatening a breakdown of all international order and law. Surely the 90 percent . . . must find some way to make their will prevail. . . . It seems to be unfortunately true that the epidemic of world lawlessness is spreading. And mark this well! When an epidemic of physical disease starts to spread, the community approves and joins in a quarantine of the patients in order to protect the health of the community against the spread of the disease.

Such a quarantine against aggressor nations was his prescription for maintaining peace in the increasingly precarious international order.

The worsening international situation also aroused alarm in Congress. In consultation with the president, the lawmakers reluctantly voted to embark on a military preparedness program. Throughout the Depression Congress had made only minimal appropriations for the armed forces. Between 1933 and 1937 appropriations had averaged only about $180 million annually. The navy—a favorite of Roosevelt's—fared much better than the army, which numbered no more than 110,000 officers and men. In fact, the army was so poverty stricken that its men were forced to drill with wooden rifles. The Military Appropriations Act of 1938 changed all this as Congress voted $1 billion to expand the armed forces. A strong America, Roosevelt declared, would be the best deterrent against a would-be aggressor:

> The American nation is committed to peace and the principal reason for the existence of our armed forces is to guarantee our peace. The army of the United States is one of the smallest in the world. However . . . its efficiency is steadily improving.

Amid American rearmament preparations in 1938 and 1939, the political situation in Europe worsened. At the Munich Conference of 1938 British Prime Minister Neville Chamberlain and French

Premier Edward Daladier abjectly surrendered to Hitler's demand for the annexation of the Sudetenland. In March 1939 German troops invaded Czechoslovakia while its British and French allies stood impotently by. In Spain Franco won a decisive victory over the Republicans and established a harsh fascist dictatorship. Mussolini was preparing to move Italian troops into Albania and Greece, to give himself a foothold in the Balkans. And in September 1939 Nazi troops attacked Poland, which they subdued and occupied within a month. The invasion of Poland left England and France little choice but to resist, and on September 3, 1939, World War II officially began.

Most Americans were still hopeful that the outbreak of World War II in Europe would not lead to significant changes in the Roosevelt Administration's policy of nonintervention. Only in later years did Americans come to realize that the war ended the isolationism in United States diplomacy. Throughout the 1930s the Depression was a major influence on foreign relations. Disillusionment after World War I had strengthened the isolationist mood, but the Depression led Americans to be even more concerned with domestic than foreign problems. Increasing helplessness of the League of Nations during the 1930s, as well as the outbreak of armed hostilities in Europe, Africa, and the Far East, only intensified the resolve for nonintervention. Involvement of the United States in international crises was considered to be as detrimental to the national interest in the 1930s as United States intervention supposedly had been in the First World War. As President Roosevelt often said, the great enemy which Americans had to fight was the Depression. The year 1939 found the United States in a rapidly changing world. The Nazi menace to western civilization was replacing the Depression as the overriding issue in American public life. American policymakers found themselves increasingly devoting time to foreign affairs rather than to domestic issues.

CHAPTER 9

America's Road to War, 1939–1941

Although eventual American participation in the global conflict appeared likely, most Americans still hoped to avoid it. That question was resolved by Japan's attack on Pearl Harbor, on December 7, 1941. By then most Americans were more prepared for war—psychologically as well as militarily—than they had been two years earlier. Between 1939 and 1941 the problems of the nation—and its mood—changed dramatically.

WORLD WAR II IN EUROPE

In a brilliant display of military skill and power, the Germans had conducted a *Blitzkrieg* (lightning war) that caused the Poles to surrender within a month as the French and British stood by. Also in 1939 the Germans signed a friendship pact with the Soviet Union which appeared to eliminate possible Russian opposition in the east. The German army stationed on the Franco-German border remained inactive during the winter of 1939–1940. Indeed, some observers concluded rather prematurely that this *Sitzkrieg* (sit-down war) was phony.

Unfortunately, a series of German advances in spring 1940 indicated unmistakably that this conflict was anything but phony. Powerful German armies subdued Norway and Denmark in April. Within weeks of the Scandinavian operation, German forces swept into Belgium, Holland, and France, quickly crushing all opposition and occupying all three. To the dismay of Americans, France surrendered on June 22, 1940, leaving only the British to carry on the struggle against the Germans. Wherever the Nazis extended their New Order, they established an unprecedented and barbaric reign of terror. Concentration and forced labor camps, executions of civilians, extreme brutality, and massive looting became the hallmarks of German occupation. Now that Hitler was, in effect, the master of Europe, his earlier promises to extend his New Order to the rest of the world were taken more seriously.

Hitler was at this time planning the invasion of England. At one time his plans were set for 1940, but the action was postponed until the following year. In the fall of 1940 the German Luftwaffe began the Battle of Britain. Large-scale bombing attacks preceded what was to be a direct invasion. On almost every night between September 1940 and March 1941, hundreds of German planes swept over Great Britain, raining thousands of bombs on British cities in an attempt to demoralize the civilian population. Yet, the English people maintained high morale and stubbornly defied the German onslaught.

Hitler changed his mind about invading England when he decided to go after his most hated foe, the Soviet Union. Before he began a Russian campaign in 1941, however, he came to the aid of the Italians, who were suffering serious reverses at the hands of Albanian guerrillas and the Greek army. Hitler sent German forces into the Balkans, and within a few months subdued Yugoslavia, Greece, Hungary, Rumania, and Bulgaria, while simultaneously challenging the British in North Africa.

In June more than forty German divisions began a major invasion of the Soviet Union. Within a few months they had penetrated deep into its interior and were almost within sight of Moscow.

By the end of 1941 Germany appeared on the road to world domination, having conquered most of Europe in less than two years and having penetrated the depths of the Soviet Union. Americans could not help but be concerned about their own fate.

PREPAREDNESS: MOBILIZING AMERICA'S RESOURCES

President Roosevelt was keenly sensitive to the dangers that Nazi world domination held for the United States. Late in 1938 he sent Bernard Baruch, a financier and former director of the War Industries Board who had supervised America's economic mobilization effort during World War I, on a fact-finding mission. He brought back alarming news. Germany appeared invincible, Baruch reported. Its rearmament program had made it the strongest military power in the world. In 1938 the German air force could boast of 3,353 planes compared to 1,900 for the Soviet Union—and only 1,600 for the United States. Baruch urged a rapid build-up of American military might as the best possible deterrent to attack.

With his worst fears thus confirmed, Roosevelt asked Congress to increase defense appropriations. Baruch advocated expenditures on a scale exceeding $3 billion annually—a sum also advocated by the influential Assistant Secretary for War Louis Johnson. Isolationists in Congress still opposed any but the most minimal expenditures. Roosevelt once again took a middle ground between the two extremes.

A modest rearmament effort was begun, although Roosevelt spoke more strongly to Congress about the need to rearm:

> We have learned that survival cannot be guaranteed by arming after the attack begins . . . that long before any overt military act, aggression begins with preliminaries of propaganda. . . . All about us rage undeclared wars—military and economic. All about us grow more deadly armaments—military and economic. All about us are threats of new aggression—military and economic.
>
> The world has grown so small, and weapons of attack so swift, that no nation can be safe in its will to peace so long as any other single powerful nation refuses to settle its grievances at the council table. We . . . must have armed forces and defenses strong enough to ward off sudden attack against strategic positions and key facilities.

In response Congress appropriated $525 million to be divided between the army, navy, and the fledgling air force. In addition, the president was authorized to stockpile essential materials. The Stockpile Act of 1939 allocated $125 million for this purpose. Meanwhile, the Educational Orders Act the same year was designed to bring greater coordination between military planners and their industrial suppliers. This measure authorized expenditures of $2 billion yearly to enable the War Department to familiarize key contractors with particular kinds of munitions and other supplies needed. Assistant Secretary of War Louis Johnson sponsored scores of conferences at which he acquainted manufacturers in diverse industries with specific problems expected in large-scale industrial mobilization.

Since the industrial potential of the nation in case of war was really not known in 1939, Roosevelt also created a new advisory agency, the War Resources Board, established in August 1939 as a civilian advisory commission to the Army-Navy Munitions Board. Its purpose was to develop a comprehensive industrial mobilization plan. Headed by Edward R. Stettinius, president of the U.S. Steel Corporation, the board included executives such as Walter Gifford of the American Telephone and Telegraph Company, John Pratt of General Motors, and Robert Wood of Sears, Roebuck Company. Roosevelt had known Stettinius's father during World War I and felt a special fondness for his son. Although staffed by impressive business leaders, the board did little more than to file a report on how industrial mobilization could be achieved. In part its ineffectiveness was due to Roosevelt's desire to maintain direct personal supervision of major portions of the defense program. To facilitate his objective, he issued an executive order on September 8, 1939, creating the Office of Emergency Management, to be set up within the White House. This allowed Roosevelt to centralize members of his staff who worked on various phases of mobilization. In addition he selected General George C. Marshall as the army's new Chief of Staff. Marshall was known to be eager to cooperate with the president and Congress, and was also sympathetic to strengthening of the armed forces. To ensure coordination of military and civilian policies, the president issued a military order requiring the Chiefs of Staff, the Aeronautics Board, and the Army-Navy Munitions Board to report directly to him rather than to respective Cabinet members. Such reorganization effectively enabled Roosevelt to supervise all aspects of defense policy and facilitated coordination between civilian and military officials. Most important, Roosevelt was able to create any emergency agencies needed for national security. By 1939, then, the president had begun the process of creating an organizational structure to harness the nation's military and industrial potential in case of war.

Yet Roosevelt shrank from adopting any far-sweeping comprehensive plan for industrial mobilization. Throughout 1939 and 1940 Bernard Baruch urged him to accept a detailed blueprint for centralized industrial mobilization such as one he had devised during World War I. And although Roosevelt professed to be sympathetic to Baruch, he was, in fact, as temperamentally opposed to an abstract scheme for mobilization as he was to abstract ideologies. He also hoped to avoid a push for intervention, opposed by so many Americans, until after the presidential election in 1940. Moreover, his political sense persuaded him that he a one should retain the major reins of power over civilian as well as mi tary mobilization. Consequently, the preparedness program between 1 39 and 1941 was as piecemeal and experimental as was the New Deal f om 1933 to 1935. Unfortunately, this resulted in waste and duplication that hampered rearmament in 1939 and 1940. On the other hand, it allowed the Administration to be flexible and to deal with new or unforeseen needs. Moreover, it permitted a wide range of interest groups in the nation to have a voice in shaping the defense program. Such participation aroused an enthusiasm and high morale among Americans that a more rigid plan might have been unable to tap.

Production of military goods increased somewhat in the United States during the first year of the war. Americans delivered 2,300 planes to the Allies, as well as small quantities of tanks and other weapons. Even so, some of Roosevelt's critics—Charles A. Lindbergh among them—accused him of being a warmonger.

The fall of France in 1940 prior to the American election provided the shock that convinced an increasing number of Americans to support an acceleration of the defense program. In June and July 1940 Congress readily acceded to President Roosevelt's request for additional funds to rearm the nation by appropriating more than $8 billion. Congress also authorized a one-year military draft. At the same time Roosevelt broadened the political complexion of his cabinet by appointing two prominent Republicans to key positions. As his Secretary of War he chose Henry L. Stimson who had directed the

Department of State under Herbert Hoover. To head the Navy Department he selected Frank Knox, a Chicago newspaper publisher who had been the Republican vice-presidential candidate in 1936. A Gallup poll at the time indicated that at least one half of the American public approved of these measures, reflecting a gradual shift of public opinion away from isolation.

Roosevelt now also sought to accelerate the pace of industrial production. During the first half of 1940 many industries had lagged behind in the shift to manufacture of war supplies. To some extent this was due to the Administration's lack of leadership in guiding business and agriculture, but it was also due to serious shortages of essential materials such as aviation gasoline, electric power, and railway freight cars. In May of 1940, thus, Roosevelt fell back on the World War I experience and appointed a Council of National Defense, composed mostly of cabinet members. He appointed William S. Knudsen, president of General Motors, chairman and instructed him to produce 50,000 planes. Almost immediately Knudsen began to award large defense contracts that averaged about $1.5 billion monthly. Meanwhile, Congress authorized the Reconstruction Finance Corporation to finance the building of new war plants and to stockpile supplies such as rubber and scarce metals.

Shortages continued to hamper various industries, leading Roosevelt to take still more emergency measures. He also established a Priorities Board attached to the Council of National Defense; it had authority to require manufacturers to place war orders before civilian production orders. He created the Office of Production Management to allocate scarce goods and raw materials and to schedule military requirements. William S. Knudsen and Sidney Hillman, a labor leader prominent in the CIO, were appointed co-directors. To control inflation as well as to ration scarce civilian goods, the president established the Office of Price Administration—largely to protect consumers. During the second half of 1940, therefore, American industry began to hum; it entered a production boom such as the nation had not witnessed for over a decade. By the end of the year 17,000 planes, 9,000 tanks, and 17,000 heavy guns had rolled off assembly lines.

In the middle of this industrial push and the deteriorating world situation, the major political parties assembled in the summer of 1940 to select their presidential candidates. The Republicans met first, just two days after the French surrendered to Germany. In a crisis atmosphere, staunch isolationists such as Senators Robert Taft (Ohio), and Hiram Johnson (California), who opposed American aid to the allies, fought to a deadlock with internationalists like Thomas E. Dewey of New York. In a series of surprise moves, the internationalists won control of the convention and nominated Wendell Willkie, a relatively unknown figure. A Democrat until 1933, Willkie was president of one of the South's major public utility corporations, Commonwealth and Southern. Like Roosevelt, Willkie was sympathetic to the Allied cause and, in fact, privately believed that American involvement in the war might be difficult to avoid.

Among the Democrats, speculation was rife that Roosevelt would accept the nomination for a third time. Roosevelt had said little about his political intentions, yet he did not encourage other candidates or do anything to restrain his supporters. When the Democrats met in July 1940, Roosevelt sent them a message that implied that he would accept the nomination if it were offered—a gesture that was in itself sufficient to start a Roosevelt bandwagon. Although he lost the support of some leading Democrats, such as his former manager James A. Farley, the convention nominated him with great enthusiasm, conscious that they were breaking the two-term precedent.

The campaign was bitter. Willkie attacked Roosevelt for being power hungry. He criticized the slowness and haphazardness of Roosevelt's defense program. Although an active interventionist himself, Willkie, in the last weeks before the election, accused Roosevelt of being a warmonger. Roosevelt did not respond to Willkie's charges until late in the campaign. Then he reiterated his record and his experience, leaving it to his partisans to tell the voters that they should not swap horses in midstream in a time of world crisis. That strategy worked, for in 1940 Roosevelt received 27 million votes, compared to 22 million for Willkie.

By the end of 1940 the nation's defense program was finally gathering momentum. During the first year of the European war, the president had not established a clearly defined mobilization plan.

Always eager to protect his political position, he shrank from decisive action—in particular, he was anxious to offend neither the isolationists nor the noninterventionists. Only after the fall of France in June 1940 did Roosevelt communicate his alarm to the nation and solicit support for a large-scale national defense program. Then, confident of the approval of a majority of the American people, he embarked on a more determined course by pledging maximum aid—short of war—to the Allies.

FROM ISOLATION TO INTERVENTION

The fall of France brought World War II closer to America. Any illusions which Americans might have cherished concerning Nazi intentions about world conquest or about the strength of the Allies were rudely shattered by the spectacular German victories. England alone stood between the United States and the Nazi juggernaut—and the British showed obvious signs of weakening. Americans were now forced to confront the realities of the war as it affected their own national interest.

The reversal in the United States' position was publicized by the president in his commencement speech at the University of Virginia on June 10, 1940, as France fell, when he said:

> Some indeed still hold to the now somewhat obvious delusion that we of the United States can safely permit the United States to become a lone island, a lone island in a world dominated by the philosophy of force.
>
> Such an island may be the dream of those who still talk and vote as isolationists. Such an island represents to me and to the overwhelming majority of the Americans today a helpless nightmare of a people without freedom. Yes, the nightmare of a people lodged in prison, handcuffed, hungry, and fed through the bars from day to day by the contemptuous, unpitying masters of other continents.
>
> Let us not hesitate—all of us—to proclaim certain truths. Overwhelmingly, we as a nation . . . we are convinced that military and naval victory of the gods of force and hate would endanger the institutions of democracy in the Western world—and that, equally, therefore, the whole of our sympathies lie with those nations that are giving the lifeblood of combat against those forces.

In our unity . . . we will pursue two obvious and simultaneous courses; we will extend to the opponents of force the material resources of this nation, and at the same time we will harness and speed up the use of those resources in order that we ourselves in the Americas may have equipment and training equal to the task of any emergency and every defense.

Americans could no longer be absolutely impartial but must extend all aid to the Allies short of war, Roosevelt felt. The collapse of France had created a threat to American security in the Caribbean too. The French possessions of Martinique and Guadeloupe were in strategic locations and might possibly be occupied by Germans. To counter this danger, the Roosevelt Administration called for a meeting of Pan-American foreign ministers to meet in Havana in late July 1940. This conference displayed surprising unanimity, for large numbers of German settlers and their descendants in Argentina, Brazil, and Chile had cultivated considerable pro-German sentiment in South America. In a Declaration of Havana the participating nations declared that they would consider an attack on any one American country an attack on all. A commission was established to take temporary control of any European possessions in the Western Hemisphere to guard against possible incursions by the Axis.

During spring and summer of 1940, British Prime Minister Winston Churchill was importuning Roosevelt to transfer some U.S. naval vessels to desperately needed convoy duty in the North Atlantic. When Churchill first broached the question, Roosevelt was decidedly negative, although Churchill argued that England had lost one-third of its fleet of one hundred destroyers, and that those remaining were needed to repel the expected German invasion from the east. "We must ask therefore, as a matter of life or death," wrote Churchill, "to be reinforced with these destroyers." Roosevelt hesitated to act without congressional approval. In July the British ambassador to the United States, Lord Lothian, offered the United States the rights to military bases in Newfoundland, Bermuda, and Trinidad in return for aid. The idea of a trade had greater appeal to Roosevelt. Through his journalist friend William Allen White, he sounded out the Republican challenger Wendell Willkie on his attitude toward the proposal. Willkie agreed not to make it an issue. Meanwhile, a group of distinguished lawyers advised the president that he did not require congressional approval for a destroyer transfer, and in early fall

Roosevelt transferred fifty antiquated World War I destroyers to Great Britain in return for eight American military bases in the New World. Public reaction to the transaction was mostly favorable, in part because Roosevelt had cultivated it carefully during the preceding months.

While Americans were going to the polls in the fall of 1940, the English were huddling in bomb shelters and wondering about the impending bankruptcy of their government. Great Britain had spent $4.5 billion of its $6.5 billion in dollar reserves, and lacked funds to pay for further large-scale purchases of military supplies in the United States. British Prime Minister Churchill chose to present his case dramatically. As Roosevelt was vacationing in the Caribbean on a navy cruiser in early December, a seaplane approached the vessel, bearing an urgent message from Churchill. "My dear Mr. President," he wrote, "As we reach the end of this year, I feel you will expect me to lay before you the prospects for 1941. I do so with candor and confidence, because it seems to me that the vast majority of American citizens have recorded their conviction that the safety of the United States, as well as the future of our two Democracies and the kind of civilization for which they stand, is bound up with the survival and independence of the British Commonwealth of Nations, . . . [But] the moment approaches when we shall no longer be able to pay cash for shipping and other supplies. . . . Regard this letter not as an appeal for aid but as a statement of minimum action to achieve our common purpose." Churchill urged Roosevelt to provide supplies the British so desperately needed but for which they could no longer pay.

Roosevelt considered the appeal and then formulated a plan of action. After he returned to Washington and consulted with his aides, he revealed his scheme for what became known as the Lend-Lease Program. At a press conference he told reporters: "What I'm trying to do is to eliminate the dollar sign, . . . get rid of the silly, foolish old dollar sign. Well, let me give you an illustration: Suppose my neighbor's home catches on fire, and I have a length of garden hose four or five hundred feet away. If he can take my garden hose and connect it with his hydrant, I may help him to put out his fire. Now what do I do? I don't say to him before that operation, 'Neighbor, my garden hose cost me $15; you have to pay me $15 for it.' What is the transaction that goes on? I don't want $15—I want my garden hose back after the fire is over. All right, if it goes through the fire all right, intact . . . he gives it back to me and thanks me very much for the use of it."

On December 29, 1940, Roosevelt spoke to Americans directly in a fireside chat. "The United States," he said, "must be the great arsenal of democracy." He asked Congress for authority to send war supplies to England in return for goods and services rather than for dollars. His pleas fell on sympathetic ears, and within two months Congress appropriated $7 billion for operation of the Lend-Lease Program. In return for supplies the British also made additional air and naval bases available to the United States off the Canadian coast and in the British West Indies.

The Havana Declaration, together with Roosevelt's commencement address at the University of Virginia and the adoption of Lend-Lease, transformed the United States from a neutral into a partisan, albeit nonbelligerent, nation. This new diplomatic status was developed further by Roosevelt's authorization of limited American naval action in the first half of 1941. By then an increasing number of Americans began to realize that England was America's first line of defense. If England were defeated, no doubt the United States would be left to face Nazi Germany alone. American public opinion was shifting in favor of intervention. Since Roosevelt kept a close watch on opinions expressed in the popular press, he felt more assured in modifying the nation's neutral stance. In view of the great shipping losses the British suffered in the Atlantic at the hands of German submarines, in March 1941 Roosevelt authorized American shipyards to repair British vessels. In addition he ordered the transfer of ten Coast Guard cutters to the Royal Navy for convoy duty. And he extended the American Neutrality Patrol almost 2,000 miles into the Atlantic. The U.S. Navy was ordered to locate German submarines but not to attack them.

By the middle of 1941 Roosevelt extended American non-belligerency further. Fleets of Nazi submarines were roaming in the North Atlantic, sinking British vessels at an alarming rate of two ships daily and endangering the American supply route to England. With the United States now committed to the defense of Great Britain, the president felt compelled to take additional steps to ensure the continued flow of aid to the embattled English. That lifeline seemed threatened by a German declaration in March 1941 extending the Atlantic war zone to include Iceland as well as the Denmark Strait between Greenland and Iceland. The practical effect of this measure was that German submarines and surface vessels would roam Atlantic waters less than a thousand miles from American shores. Roosevelt considered the German action for several months before making retaliatory moves. In July 1941 he announced that U.S. Marines would occupy Iceland to prevent its possible seizure by Germany, and to ensure the defense of the Western Hemisphere. These measures made the United States a *de facto* ally of the British.

Although Roosevelt and Churchill were in almost daily contact in 1940 and 1941, the two leaders had not met personally. Roosevelt recalled having seen Churchill briefly during World War I, but the British leader could not remember the occasion. Consequently, in July 1941 Harry Hopkins went to London to arrange a secret meeting. Within a few weeks Churchill embarked on one of the Royal Navy's finest battleships bound for Argentia, off Newfoundland. Roosevelt was steaming to the rendezvous on the U.S. Navy cruiser *Augusta*. The two men met aboard the American ship on August 9, 1941. Churchill hoped to secure some kind of commitment from the United States to participate in the war, but Roosevelt refused to bind his nation in this way. The military advisors who accompanied the two men did discuss loose plans for Anglo-American cooperation at some future time, if circumstances warranted.

The outcome of this meeting was the Atlantic Charter, a joint declaration concerning common aims. This document embodied an Anglo-American vision for organization of the post-war world. That world was to be ordered according to principles based on self-determination of nations. The charter also reiterated Anglo-American adherence to the Four Freedoms which Roosevelt had enunciated in his annual message to Congress earlier that year—freedom from want, freedom from fear, freedom of speech, and freedom of religion. When the contents of the Atlantic Charter were made public a week after the meeting, Americans responded positively. In the context of growing support for his diplomacy, the president extended Lend-Lease aid to Russia a few months later.

By fall 1941 the United States was involved in an undeclared naval war. On September 4, 1941, a German submarine had attacked the U.S. destroyer *Greer* off Iceland. President Roosevelt reacted by ordering U.S. naval vessels to shoot on sight any German or Italian vessels they encountered in the North Atlantic. A few weeks later Congress approved the arming of American merchant ships.

Throughout 1940 and 1941 Roosevelt's shift to a diplomacy tending to intervention came under fire from various groups and individuals. Staunch isolationists such as Senator Burton Wheeler of Montana belittled the supposed threat from the Axis powers and castigated Roosevelt as a warmonger. Some Americans, such as Charles Lindbergh, also did not regard fascism as a threat to the United States and opposed Roosevelt's policies of aiding the Allies. There were also ethnic isolationists such as Americans of German or Irish descent, antimilitarists, left-wingers, and Communists. Early in 1941 the opponents of intervention organized the America First Committee. Through an active public relations campaign and lobbying in Congress, the committee brought its views before the American public, although international events increasingly weakened its influence.

On the other hand, the advocates of intervention felt that Roosevelt was too slow and cautious in extending aid to the Allies. Led by William Allen White, a well-known newspaper editor from Kansas, they organized the Committee to Defend America by Aiding the Allies to counter the influence of isolationists and to prod the Administration into closer collaboration with France and Britain. Despite these organizations neither the isolationists nor the interventionists swayed large numbers of Americans as effectively as the rapidly changing military situation in Europe and the Far East. The majority of Americans, however, were still holding out hope that direct participation in the war by the United States might not be necessary.

While Roosevelt had his hands full in dealing with the European crisis after 1939, American relations with Japan were also deteriorating. Despite protests by the United States, the Japanese continued their invasion of China, begun in 1937. One of the Japanese government's major objectives during this period was an alliance with Nazi Germany, which promised to facilitate further expansion in Asia. After tortuous negotiations Japan concluded the Tri-Partite

Agreement with Germany and Italy in 1940. Japan recognized German and Italian dominance in Europe, and the European powers agreed to recognize Japanese influence in East Asia. They also promised to aid the Japanese if they were attacked by a neutral power. Such an alliance was clearly a challenge to the United States, since American insistence on Japanese recognition of the Open Door Policy and the independence of China was a cloak for allowing the United States to maintain a dominant position in East Asia and to limit Japanese expansion there. The goals of the United States and Japan were now on a collision course.

On hearing of British recognition of Japanese conquests in China, in July 1939, Roosevelt warned Japan that he might impose embargoes on the export of raw materials such as steel, iron, and petroleum. Initially, the response of the Japanese government was restrained; but in the spring of 1940, Nazi victories in Europe emboldened the Japanese. A more militant government headed by Prime Minister Konoye came to power in July. Its military leaders decided the time was ripe to seize French Indo-China and the Dutch East Indies, now that Japan had become an Axis partner. That such moves would further antagonize the United States was clear. When the Japanese made incursions into Indo-China in July and December, Roosevelt reacted by placing embargoes on the export of aviation gasoline, scrap metals, and other vital materials to Japan. Furious, the Japanese were willing to bide their time in order to bolster their military prowess.

Within the framework of their respective aspirations, neither the leaders of the United States nor of Japan felt in 1941 that they could make significant concessions. During April and May the Konoye government offered various proposals to Washington, including the suggestion that the United States and Japan enter into a neutrality pact. Among other things, such a pact would allow the Japanese to seize British, French, and Dutch possessions in Asia. They also suggested a personal meeting between President Roosevelt and Prime Minister Konoye to attempt to settle their differences.

After the German invasion of Russia in June 1941, the Japanese became bolder and occupied the southern portion of French Indo-

China. Roosevelt was furious. In July 1941 he closed the Panama Canal to Japanese shipping, impounded Japanese funds in the United States, and extended the embargo to include additional raw materials. Both sides were now taking firmer and more intransigent positions from which retreat was increasingly difficult. Konoye invited Roosevelt to a conference to discuss mutual problems, but the president, heeding the advice of his Secretary of State, declined to attend unless the Japanese first recognized China's independence. This unwillingness to compromise strengthened the position of militarists in Japan, and in September 1941 they began to make secret war preparations. In October the aggressive militarist Hideki Tojo became the new prime minister. Although negotiations continued throughout October and November, rigid and opposing positions of General Tojo and Secretary Hull doomed them to failure.

During the last week of November 1941, American intelligence sources surmised that Japanese military leaders were preparing for an attack on either American or Allied possessions. The departments of army and navy sent warnings to commanders in the Pacific indicating that Japanese troop and naval movements suggested possible attacks on Guam or the Philippines. No one knew precisely where the Japanese might strike, especially since American intelligence operations were still uncoordinated and frequently channeled confused information to various agencies in Washington. Since many American military men expected an attack on British territories in Singapore or Malaya, they were not overly concerned about other areas. In Hawaii Admiral Husband E. Kimmel concentrated the Pacific fleet at Pearl Harbor largely to minimize sabotage. General Walter C. Short rather casually dispersed his forces in the Hawaiian Islands. Thus, the United States was caught off-guard when a Japanese carrier task force loosed the first wave of 189 planes on American naval vessels and on air fields at Pearl Harbor, Hawaii. Neither this nor a second wave of 171 planes met significant opposition as they attacked the American fleet. All eight U.S. battleships in Oahu harbor were disabled; three cruisers and three destroyers were blown out of the water; and virtually all American planes on the ground were destroyed. Other Japanese forces simultaneously were attacking the Philippines, Hong

Kong, Siam, Malaya, and Wake and Midway Islands. Only after the attack did the world receive the news that Japan had declared war on the United States and Great Britain.

On December 8, 1941, President Roosevelt appeared before a tense Congress to ask for a declaration of war against Japan:

> Yesterday, December 7, 1941—a date which will live in infamy—the United States of America was suddenly and deliberately attacked by naval and air forces of the empire of Japan.
>
> As Commander-in-Chief of the Army and Navy, I have directed that all measures be taken for our defense, that always will our whole nation remember the character of the onslaught against us.
>
> No matter how long it may take us to overcome this premeditated invasion, the American people in their righteous might, will win through to absolute victory.
>
> With confidence in our armed forces, with the unbounding determination of our people, we will gain the inevitable triumph, so help us God.

Within a few days Germany and Italy also declared war on the United States. Americans were now engaged in another worldwide conflict.

Despite the desire of an overwhelming majority of the American people to remain aloof from the war in Europe, by 1941 the United States was once again embroiled in a major conflict. Between 1939 and 1941 circumstances narrowed the alternatives open to American policymakers. Keeping a close pulse on public opinion, President Roosevelt had followed a restrained neutrality until June of 1940. The fall of France, however, shocked Americans into an acute awareness of what a Nazi victory in Western Europe would mean and led them to support a policy of extensive aid. But at the time of Pearl Harbor the reasons for United States entry into the war were clear to most Americans. Nazi and Japanese policies were restricting American commercial expansion in Europe and the Far East. The proliferation of Nazi and other totalitarian governments constituted an increasing threat to democracy in the United States and elsewhere. Ultimately the ideals of freedom and of the Christian-Judeo ethic were being challenged by Nazi doctrines of racial superiority and barbarism.

World War II was not fought primarily because of disputes over territories, economic concessions, or political rivalries, although these played a role. From the American point of view the conflict was generated by the clash of two radically differing ideologies and life-styles. This became a war for survival.

CHAPTER 10

Restructuring the World Order: Military and Diplomatic Policies, 1941–1945

World War II transformed Roosevelt into a world leader. Although many domestic issues remained unsettled, the nation's major problems between 1941 and 1945 revolved around the war. As commander in chief, Roosevelt assumed the heavy burdens of directing military as well as diplomatic policies at the highest level. It was his responsibility to supervise military build-up and to determine the most effective deployment of America's military might. It was also his task to formulate foreign policy goals and to conduct delicate negotiations with neutral nations as well as with war-time allies.

The attack on Pearl Harbor plunged the United States into global war. Americans were compelled to fight five wars simultaneously. The war in the Pacific—in the Philippines, New Guinea, Midway, and Guam—was foremost in the minds of most Americans right after Pearl Harbor. At the same time, however, a fierce naval war raged in the North Atlantic, where German submarines exacted a costly toll on American and Allied shipping. Within a year Americans also became involved in the campaign against the Germans in North Africa—and soon thereafter played a major role in the invasion of Italy. Once the United States and the Allies entered France in 1944 to strike at Germany directly, Americans also became involved in a major military operation in western and central Europe.

FDR'S MILITARY POLICIES

The supervision of these extensive military operations was a herculean task. Roosevelt performed the arduous duties of commander in chief with the same relish with which he had wielded executive powers during the New Deal. He sought to balance military, political, and economic considerations with exigencies of the world situation. Such balancing required the artful handling of military and civilian individuals and groups. The juggling of these myriad divergent interests placed great pressures on the president, yet outwardly he continued to be calm and affable.

FDR's personality profoundly affected his performance during the war. A connoisseur of power, he relished the extraordinary expansion of his authority as he assumed his constitutional duties as commander in chief. Secretary of State Hull later noted that FDR took special pride in this role, and indeed—at state dinners in the White House—preferred to be introduced as commander in chief rather than as president. During World War I Roosevelt had been deeply frustrated by his inability to participate in active service in France since he was serving as Assistant Secretary of the Navy; in World War II he hoped to participate fully in military planning. He wanted to act as coordinator, mediator, and compromiser. Despite this, Roosevelt maintained his usual independence. In 1942 Roosevelt overrode the advice of most of his military commanders, who favored greater emphasis on the war against Japan. Instead he authorized large-scale American involvement in the Allied invasion of North Africa. Roosevelt also insisted on the *unconditional* surrender of the Axis powers, although some of his critics argued that it could prolong German resistance. In opposition to British Prime Minister Winston Churchill, Roosevelt favored the opening of a second front in France rather than in the Balkans. Churchill felt that this would open central and eastern Europe to Soviet influence.

Roosevelt's first priority, however, was a quick military victory, and he felt that a new French front was the way to achieve it. Unlike the British or Russians, he was less inclined to give primacy to long-range political objectives to be attained after the fighting stopped. Mostly, he and other Americans wanted and expected a quick end to the war.

FDR maintained close relationships with his military leaders. His personal contacts with Chief of Staff General George C. Marshall were as cordial as those with Admiral of the Fleet Ernest King and Air Force General Hap Arnold. If he had relatively few serious policy disagreements with these men, this was largely because of the mutual respect they felt for one another. There was little turnover in the American high command during war time.

Without question Roosevelt's wartime mobilization shaped the creation of a military-industrial complex whose influence was to persist and grow after World War II. Effective mobilization required a closely coordinated effort between business, industry, and military and government officials. Such cooperation was characteristic of President Wilson's economic mobilization in World War I, in which Roosevelt himself had played an integral role. During the war close relations between business and government multiplied manifold. Entire cities such as Knoxville, Tennessee; Los Alamos, New Mexico; or Hanford, Washington, became largely dependent on national security expenditures. In this fashion, the war years fostered the growth of a military-industrial complex in the United States. Unwittingly perhaps, President Roosevelt created the organizational structure in which this military-industrial complex—an intricate network of relationships between individuals in industry, the military, and government—was to flourish. As the Chief Executive himself noted in 1943, Dr. New Deal had retired to become Dr. Win-the-War.

World War II mobilization resulted in the establishment of the largest American military force in the nation's history. By 1944 the army had mobilized more than 12 million men and women into an awesome striking force. The navy was at peak strength, consisting of more than 3,408,000 men and women, the largest naval force in the world. And the air force, with fewer than 300 planes in 1939, had more than 60,000 aircraft just five years later.

THE WAR FRONTS, 1941-1945

The price of victory was not as cheap as many Americans expected it would be at the time of Pearl Harbor. Indeed, the first year of the war was characterized mainly by retreat. Only by 1943 were American and Allied forces able to mount offensives, and not until 1944 was military triumph over Germany and Japan in sight.

The military situation early in 1942 was grim. In the Pacific, the Japanese appeared to be sweeping all before them. They overran the oil-rich Netherlands East Indies, fortified the jungles of New Guinea, and took control of Burma and hundreds of small islands in the central and south Pacific, including the Gilbert Islands, Guam, Wake Island, and Singapore. In well executed campaigns the Japanese defeated American forces in the Philippines. Outnumbered and isolated from supplies, American army and naval units fought a valiant but losing battle under Generals Douglas MacArthur and Jonathan M. Wainwright. By May 1942 the Japanese broke the last American Resistance on the islands. They forced their prisoners to submit to the grueling Bataan Death March, which ended in their confinement in prison camps, and gloated over General Wainwright's surrender. On the seas, Japanese naval squadrons destroyed an Allied fleet at the Battle of the Java Sea (February 27, 1942). In subsequent naval engagements—the Battle of the Coral Sea (May 7, 1942) and the Battle of Midway (June 4, 1942)—American forces were able to contain the Japanese tide and to inflict losses. The stunning first year of the Pacific War dispelled the illusion of some Americans that defeat of the Japanese would be quick and easy.

At the same time the United States Navy was preoccupied with the menace of German submarines in the Atlantic. During most of 1942 packs of U-boats roamed along the American sea lanes to England, sinking about three ships daily—or more than one thousand vessels yearly. The rate of ship destruction was at least three times as great as the ability of United States shipyards to replace them. And as the flow of American supplies to England increased in 1942, the navy found itself short on escort vessels to protect the long streams of Allied convoys through the North Atlantic. Throughout 1942 the navy and the shipbuilders and repairers grappled with this serious crisis in the North Atlantic.

In Europe and the Middle East, Nazi forces advanced relentlessly. German armies penetrated deep into the interior of the Soviet Union. Throughout occupied France, the Low countries, and Norway and Denmark, the Germans solidified their military stronghold. In Lybia the German Afrika Korps under German General Erwin Rommel drove back Allied armies and threatened to seize the Suez Canal—the British lifeline for oil and other essential supplies.

The tide of battle turned slowly in 1943 and 1944, when the United States and the Allies, bolstered by the American production effort, started to take the offensive. Beginning in August 1942, the navy and the marines began costly campaigns to recapture the Pacific from well-entrenched, determined Japanese forces. A campaign to oust the Japanese from the Aleutian Islands in the Northern Pacific began in May 1943; that November U.S. Marines fought bitterly to recapture the Gilbert Islands; February, 1944 found them in assault on the Marshall Islands, on hundreds of tiny atolls in the region, and in the steamy hot jungles of New Guinea. Meanwhile, the United States Navy developed various methods to combat the German submarines in the Atlantic. By use of special air patrols and newly developed radar devices, detection became easier. The navy sunk 237 German submarines in 1943. And American shipyards were now producing vast quantities of ships and escort vessels which provided necessary protection for convoys. By 1943 United States shipping losses were minimal, less than 1 percent of traffic in the Atlantic.

Elsewhere the Allied position had also improved. In Europe American and British air forces carried out massive bombing attacks on German industrial areas in an effort to cripple war production. Throughout 1943 and 1944 fleets of 1,000 to 1,500 Allied bombers dotted the German skies, raining a hail of destruction on factories, railroads, and inevitably, civilian areas in Germany. In the east the Soviet Army revealed unusual strength and courage by routing the Germans during the siege of Stalingrad (November 1942 to February 1943). Not only were the Soviets able to defend the city, but they seized the initiative to begin a long, persistent campaign to drive the

Germans out of the Soviet Union. At the same time American, British and Free French forces were mounting an offensive in North Africa, where they destroyed General Rommel's army and ended the German threat to the Suez Canal (October 1942 to May 1943). Next, they crossed the Mediterranean to Sicily, and then invaded Italy directly. By the summer of 1943 the Italians withdrew from the war, although strong German resistance in northern Italy continued.

The mood of the Allies became more optimistic by early 1944. The defeat of the Axis was in the future, but the military initiative had clearly shifted to the Allies. On June 6, 1944, American and British forces under the Supreme Allied Commander General Dwight D. Eisenhower launched the long awaited D-Day from England, a massive cross-channel invasion opening a major second front in France. More than 2 million Americans waded ashore on the Normandy beachhead and marched into the interior of France. Amid much jubilation the Allies captured Paris on August 25, 1944, and then turned east toward Germany. Around Christmas German resistance grew unexpectedly fiercer and more effective. At the Battle of the Bulge in December 1944, the Allies narrowly missed being driven back by the still-powerful German army. Meanwhile the Soviet army broke German lines and by January 1945 was speeding across Poland toward the German border. In spring 1945 the Soviet armies began their invasion of Germany from the east while the American and Allied army converged on Germany from the west. General Eisenhower restrained his forces and ordered General George S. Patton to draw back from Prague, Czechoslovakia so the victorious Soviets could be first to enter Berlin. Recognizing imminent defeat, Hitler and his closest confidantes committed suicide in an underground bunker in the city just a few days before the invasion of Berlin. Most of the other leaders of Nazi Germany were in flight. The Soviets occupied Poland, Czechoslovakia, and East Germany. On May 7, 1945, a temporary German government under Admiral Karl Doenitz surrendered unconditionally. Americans wildly celebrated Victory-in-Europe Day.

The defeat of Germany enabled the United States to shift a major part of its military force to the Far East. After the recapture of the Philippines in May 1945, the consolidation of supply lines, and establishment of air bases, American strength steadily grew in the Pacific. But Chief of Staff General George C. Marshall and Pacific Commander General Douglas MacArthur believed that United States strategy required the capture of the island approaches to Japan and eventually a direct invasion of Japan itself. In view of strong Japanese resistance, they expected the war to continue for at least a year or longer after Victory in Europe, and they feared that their planned assaults would entail the loss of perhaps a million American lives. In 1944 they began a series of destructive air raids on Japan, in which hundreds of American planes rained bombs on Japanese industrial areas and cities.

As Japanese hopes for victory faded, their resistance became more ferocious. Even after much of the remaining Japanese Navy was destroyed in October 1944 in the Battle of Leyte Gulf, the Japanese Navy began a major counteroffensive designed to weaken the United States position in the Philippines. The U.S. Third and Seventh Fleets under Admirals Bull Halsey and Thomas C. Kincaid were ready for them. In a series of elaborate maneuvers, the U.S. Navy sunk three battleships and ten cruisers while sustaining only light losses themselves. In China, Burma, and on countless small islands in the Pacific, Japanese soldiers fought bitterly to the death—both theirs and that of their assailants. The Americans captured Iwo Jima in March 1945 and Okinawa in June. Both islands were strategically located to serve as bomber bases and as potential stepping stones for an invasion of the Japanese mainland. Their capture by United States marine and army forces resulted in the downfall of the Japanese militarist regime of General Tojo. Yet the war continued, and many American leaders feared it would be long and difficult.

FDR'S WORLD WAR II DIPLOMACY

World War II altered the course of American diplomacy. Whereas the national mood between 1919 and 1939 had leaned toward isolation, by 1945 wartime experience convinced a majority of Americans that world leadership, collaboration with other powers and foreign intervention provided the surest and most practical road to a lasting post-war peace. The necessities and vicissitudes of the post-war era helped to produce this metamorphosis in United States diplomacy as much as Roosevelt's leadership of the Grand Alliance.

Early in the war Roosevelt became convinced that the United States would have to take the initiative in preventing neutral nations from joining the Axis cause. Thus, he embarked on an active campaign to woo Vichy France, Spain, and Portugal. Vichy France was clearly under German influence. Nevertheless its government still controlled the bulk of the French Navy as well as important military bases in Algeria and North Africa. The authority of this collaborationist regime—headed by Marshal Henri Petain—was openly challenged by the anti-Nazi, Free French government-in-exile headquartered in London. General Charles de Gaulle was its spokesman. While Roosevelt's sympathies lay clearly with the latter, he was anxious to prevent German seizure of France's fleet and its North African possessions. Consequently, Roosevelt recognized the pro-German Vichy regime, and under the Murphy-Weygand Agreement of 1940, authorized American aid for it. His action aroused bitter hostility not only from General de Gaulle but from many other critics, yet Roosevelt achieved his goal of preventing Nazi expansion in French North Africa, thus facilitating the Allied offensive in that region during the fall of 1942.

This same kind of pragmatism colored Roosevelt's policy toward Spain. General Francisco Franco was an avowed Nazi sympathizer. Roosevelt knew that Spain's strategic location, especially its proximity to Gibraltar and its safe access to the Mediterranean Sea, was essential to Allied military operations in that region, so he labored to keep Spain from joining the Axis powers. His prime instrument was economic. A poor nation, Spain desperately needed lucrative export markets. The United States arranged to purchase a variety of Spanish exports, including more than 90 percent of its tungsten. In return the Spanish received sorely needed American petroleum supplies. Such economic diplomacy combined with the declining fortunes of the Nazis persuaded General Franco to maintain a discreet neutrality, which was of inestimable benefit to the Allied cause. Secretary of State Hull cultivated the neutrality of the Portuguese government by offering economic aid in exchange for strategic American air bases in the Azores and the Canary Islands.

American policy toward the neutrals after 1941 was certainly not isolationist; rather, Roosevelt emphasized close collaboration to maintain a neutrality that was of prime benefit to the United States.

In 1942 the United States took the lead in fashioning a Grand Alliance against the Axis. Soon after Pearl Harbor, Roosevelt announced the formation of the United Nations, to be composed of countries opposed to Axis expansion. In a Declaration of the United Nations on January 1, 1942, these nations endorsed the principles of the Atlantic Charter and pledged themselves not to conclude a separate peace. By establishing this new alliance, Roosevelt hoped to replace the defunct League of Nations and to lay the groundwork for the creation of a more effectively structured organization to maintain international order in the post-war era.

The United States developed its closest friendship with the British. In 1942 Roosevelt and Churchill established the Combined Chiefs of Staff, which included the ranking military commanders of each nation. In their many meetings they jointly decided on military strategy, planned campaigns, and allocated supplies and resources. Despite conflicts and differences of opinion, the Combined Chiefs were remarkably effective in coordinating their joint ventures. The work of the many international committees achieved a high level of successful coordination, a marked contrast to the more limited collaboration during World War I.

A large part of the American-British alliance was due to the cordial personal relationship between Roosevelt and Churchill. Although the two men had their differences—most notably over self-determination for British colonies—these were nevertheless transcended by their bonds of common interest. Both men realized that close cooperation was in the best self-interest of their respective nations. Both shared a sense of history, of the common fate of the English-speaking peoples, and of the Anglo-American tradition of democracy. And as Roosevelt admired English culture, so Churchill's American-born mother, Jenny, made him especially sensitive to American traditions. These ties were reflected in Churchill's address to Congress on December 26, 1941, when he said:

You do not, I am certain, underrate the severity of the ordeal to which you and we still have to be subjected. The forces ranged against us are enormous. They are bitter. They are ruthless. . . . They will stop at nothing. . . . We have, therefore, without doubt, a time of tribulation before us. . . . Many disappointments and unpleasant surprises await us.

We have indeed to be thankful that so much time has been granted us. If Germany had tried to invade the British Isles after the French collapse in June 1940 and if Japan had declared war on the British Empire and the United States at about the same time, no one can say what disasters and agonies might not have been our lot. But now, at the end of December 1941, our transformation from easygoing peace to total war efficiency has made very great progress. . . .

Now that we are together, now that we are linked in a righteous comradeship of arms, now that our two considerable nations, each in perfect unity, have joined all their life energies in a common resolve, a new scene opens upon which a steady light will glow and brighten. . . . Here we are together defending all that to free men is dear.

It is not given to us to peer into the mysteries of the future. Still I avow my hope and faith . . . that in the days to come the British and American people will for their own safety and for the good of all walk together in majesty, in justice, and in peace.

Throughout the war the two leaders were in close communication with each other, often on a daily basis. Churchill would send cables through the American embassy in London around 2 A.M. The embassy then sent these directly to the White House through special coding machines so that Roosevelt could read them before he went to bed. And when Churchill awoke the next morning, he would often find a response waiting from Roosevelt.

American relations with the Soviet Union were not as close as with the British. The mutual distrust that arose from the differing political stances between the Americans and the Soviets was tempered but not wholly removed by wartime exigencies requiring closer collaboration. The Soviet government muted its Communist propaganda against the western nations and paid lip service to the Atlantic Charter, and the Roosevelt Administration authorized large-scale Lend-Lease aid for the Soviets. During the war the United States sent more than $11 billion in supplies to the U.S.S.R. through the Pacific port of

Vladivostok. This aid was significant in enabling Soviet armies to repel the Nazi onslaught. Roosevelt also cultivated a closer personal relationship with Soviet Premier Joseph Stalin.

Roosevelt felt that a harmonious working collaboration between the United States and the Soviet Union was absolutely essential to a lasting post-war peace. Churchill often expressed his distrust of Roosevelt's assumption—and of Soviet motives as well—earning him Roosevelt's annoyance and Stalin's ire. The uneasy relation between the Soviets and the western powers, however, was a working part of the Grand Alliance.

In the Far East Roosevelt hoped to solidify American wartime alliances by providing extensive support for Nationalist China led by General Chiang Kai-shek. The Nationalist Chinese had been fighting the Japanese since 1937 with only moderate success, and after 1941 the United States sought to stiffen their resistance. Thus, Roosevelt authorized more than $4 billion in Lend-Lease aid to Nationalist China and also extended more than $100 million in loans. In addition the United States sent military advisors to train its army. The two nations signed various treaties in 1943, under which the United States gave up its extraterritorial rights in China, while at the same time lifting the ban on Chinese immigrants that had been in effect since 1924. Although in theory Nationalist China ranked as one of the major powers in the Grand Alliance, in fact the weakness of the Chiang Kai-shek regime led the country to play a secondary role.

World War II also provided Roosevelt with a further opportunity to solidify his Good Neighbor policy toward Latin American nations and to bring them into the Alliance against the Axis. At the Inter-American Conference at Rio de Janeiro in 1942, the nations of the Western Hemisphere, except Argentina and Chile, agreed to break diplomatic relations with the Axis. Eventually they all declared war on Germany. Meanwhile the United States secured military bases in Brazil, Cuba, Ecuador, and Panama.

Despite a strong spirit of collaboration and goodwill among the members of the Grand Alliance, invariably they also had their differences which generated international conferences at the highest level. Soon after the Allied invasion of North Africa in January 1943, British, American and Free French leaders felt the need to confer on the next steps in their strategy. They arranged to meet in Casablanca in Morocco. Roosevelt, Churchill, De Gaulle, and chief military advisors deliberated on the issues before them. After considerable discussion they agreed that Allied forces should next launch an assault on Italy. In addition they accepted Roosevelt's proposal to demand unconditional surrender from the Axis.

When the Soviet government began the slow and arduous task of driving the Nazis from inside its borders, Stalin became more insistent on the opening of a second front in the West to relieve the pressure on his forces. The issue was fraught with many complexities, and it created a divergence of views among the Allies. The United States and the Soviet Union favored an assault through France, while the British wanted to attack through the Balkans. To resolve this and lesser issues, Roosevelt, Churchill, and Stalin planned a conference. They met in November 1943 at Teheran (Stalin had insisted that he could not venture far from Moscow). On their way to Teheran, Roosevelt and Churchill stopped in Cairo to meet with Chiang Kai-shek to discuss the next phase in the war against Germany and Japan. Then the leaders of the Big Three met for the first time at the Iranian seaside resort. Amidst much pomp and ceremony, they discussed some of the major issues of wartime strategy. Roosevelt and Stalin prevailed over the dubious Churchill to agree that a second front must be opened within the coming year. They also discussed the political future of Germany and Soviet eagerness to enter the war in the Pacific. On his return, Roosevelt reported to Congress:

> I have recently returned from extensive journeyings in the region of the Mediterranean and as far as the borders of Russia. . . . At Cairo and Teheran we devoted ourselves not only to military matters . . . we devoted ourselves also to the consideration of the future, to plans for the kind of world which alone can justify all the sacrifices of this war. It was well worth travelling thousands of miles over land and sea to bring about this personal meeting with Chiang Kai-shek and Winston Churchill and Marshal Stalin.
>
> I believe, and I think I can say, the other three great nations we are fighting so magnificently to gain peace are in complete agreement that we must be prepared to keep the peace by force. If the people of Germany and Japan are made to realize thoroughly that the world is not going to let them break

out again, it is possible and, I hope, probable, that they will abandon the philosophy of aggression.

Roosevelt was encouraged by his first meeting with Stalin to believe that he and the Soviet leader could work together not only to shape wartime strategy but to lay the foundations for a post-war peace. Churchill, on the other hand, came away from Teheran with greater mistrust than ever of the Soviet leader.

Although Teheran had allowed the three leaders to take measure of each other, many issues remained unresolved. Soon after the presidential election of 1944, therefore, Roosevelt made plans to meet with Churchill and Stalin again, this time at Yalta, a Black Sea resort. With military victory almost in sight, the Big Three grappled with even thornier problems of post-war politics. Stalin was intent on expanding Soviet influence in central and eastern Europe as well as in the Far East. The western statesmen wanted to insure self-determination and democratic governments for these areas. After exploring each other's views in some detail, a series of compromises was set. Germany was not dismembered, but was divided into four zones of occupation. Poland, where Communists were vying with anti-Communists for control, was to hold national elections, albeit under the watchful eye of the occupying Soviet Army. The Soviet Union agreed to declare war on Japan at the right moment—despite doubts by some American military leaders that such action was necessary. Roosevelt took pride in persuading the Soviets to participate in the organization of the United Nations, with details to be worked out at a San Francisco conference in June 1945.

The decisions at Yalta have been argued at length over the years. Some historians believed that Roosevelt yielded too much to Stalin and thus gave the Soviets hegemony in eastern Europe. Others felt that he had succeeded in laying a groundwork for closer collaboration between the United States and the Soviet Union. The Yalta agreements constituted a bundle of compromises that seemed functional at the time but were not fully satisfactory to any one participant. More important, Yalta signaled the end of isolationism and a new post-war era of collaboration among nations for the United States.

CHAPTER 11

Mobilizing For War: Expansion of the Organizational Society, 1941–1945

American involvement in World War II greatly hastened the development of a more highly organized society in the United States. Already the crisis of Depression had brought greater centralization in government, the economy, and in social and cultural life. The war accelerated this trend.

Rarely had the American people shown such self-discipline and unity as they did during World War II. They entrusted the direction of most war-time activities to a vastly expanded federal bureaucracy; they gave whole-hearted support to a high degree of centralization in the American economy to achieve maximum production; they relaxed prejudices against minority groups for the sake of war-time unity, and they even organized their cultural activities to boost their morale. More than any previous conflict, World War II prompted an unprecedented national effort to mobilize materials and human resources for the common effort.

WAR AND AMERICAN BUREAUCRACY

Federal organization in war-time was haphazard. Roosevelt organized and reorganized countless agencies. He showed little concern for their overlapping functions. Even on an organization chart, many of the agencies made little sense to planners accustomed to the well-defined delegation of authority. Yet the cumbersome organizational machine Roosevelt created worked well, mostly because it harnessed the potential abilities of millions of Americans. Roosevelt himself was perhaps more concerned with stimulating a massive mobilization effort by the entire nation than in any administrative rationale that would explain the activity. Thus, the establishment and consolidation of particular war-time agencies tended to be haphazard, the product of short-range pressures rather than long-range planning.

Once the United States formally entered the war, Roosevelt undertook more comprehensive federal direction of the national economy. In January 1942 he created the War Production Board to supervise production and distribution of a wide range of industrial products. To direct the new agency, Roosevelt appointed Donald Nelson, who hailed from Hannibal, Missouri. Shortly after graduation from the state university as a chemist in 1912, he joined Sears, Roebuck and Company and began a long and steady climb up its corporate ladder. By 1939 he was executive vice-president of Sears and known as one of the most knowledgeable retailers in the nation.

The WPB had a stormy life, full of frustrations and conflicts. In view of its broad powers it touched on most phases of American business. Indeed, many of its critics charged that it was dominated by large corporations who received favored treatment. At the same time Nelson was extremely sensitive to the demands of military leaders, who often played a major role in determining production priorities even to the detriment of the civilian sector. Because of the flurry of frenzied efforts and intensive pressures to which the WPB was subject, confusion became one of its marked characteristics. Since Roosevelt did not grant the WPB authority to control prices, Nelson had to work with other agencies in the federal bureaucracy. His authority was often challenged. That was especially true of the Office of Price Administration (OPA), to whom the president delegated authority over prices in January 1942. From an administrative view, it was cumbersome for the Chief Executive to grant one agency the power to allocate production priorities and another the power to regulate prices. But Roosevelt felt that the existence of creative tensions between competing agencies added to their overall effectiveness. In 1943 and 1944 the OPA was under the direction of Chester Bowles, a dynamic if controversial leader. Bowles was the scion of an old New England family who graduated from Yale University in 1924 and became a journalist. In 1929 he organized his own advertising agency, Benton and Bowles, which in the course of the next decade grew to be one of the more prominent in the nation. Roosevelt knew that few men had a more intimate knowledge of consumers, businessmen, and merchandizing than Chester Bowles. The OPA's primary function was to set price ceilings for thousands of nonagricultural goods and to retard inflationary pressures so as to protect consumers. Since the WPB was seeking to placate manufacturers and producers in an effort to stimulate maximum production, its recommendations for ceiling prices were usually much higher than those stipulated by the OPA. Thus, the two agencies frequently came into conflict.

On October 3, 1942, Roosevelt created still another agency, the Office of Economic Stabilization, directed by James F. Byrnes. A former congressman from South Carolina, a U.S. senator, and a U.S. Supreme Court justice, Byrnes was a moderate and conciliatory patrician whose great prestige in Washington made him an imposing figure. In an effort to unravel production snarls and imbalances and to settle conflicts between the WPB and the Department of War, the OES concentrated on rigid control of supplies of three strategic raw materials: steel, aluminum, and copper. By stringent oversight of production, Byrnes was able to regulate the flow of finished products. In addition he had authority over manpower problems and wage levels. Despite intense pressures from farm, labor, and industrial groups, Byrnes was successful in holding down inflation so that after May 1943, it increased by no more than 1 percent.

Byrnes soon was second only to Roosevelt in authority to direct the nation's total war mobilization effort. Late in 1944 as quarrels within the War Production Board rendered it ineffective, Byrnes gained even more power when he became director of a new agency, the Office of War Mobilization and Reconversion. His responsibilities now included post-war planning, particularly the job of guiding the economy from a war to a peacetime status. In part President Wilson's refusal to plan for peace in 1919 and 1920 had precipitated depression, and in 1944 and 1945 President Roosevelt was anxious to avoid a repetition of that sad chapter in the nation's history.

The Administration did not engage in the blatant censorship or hatemongering that had been characteristic of World War I, but it exercised some war-time control over the media. To a considerable extent this control was possible because of the credibility of the newsmen who took on these major responsibilities. At the time of Pearl Harbor the president asked Byron Price—then a news editor for the Associated Press—to become director of an Office of Censorship. Its main function was to examine all letters or communications between the United States and foreign nations. Price also issued a Code of Wartime Practices for publishers and broadcasters, which banned news concerning troop movements or war casualties.

Roosevelt assigned propaganda responsibilities to the Office of War Information, which he created in 1942. One of the nation's most respected radio news commentators, Elmer Davis, served as its director. He was able to attract a sizable number of advertising executives to the agency who showed great skill in cultivating patriotism at home through radio broadcasts, pamphlets, and posters. At the same time the OWI beamed broadcasts overseas to sustain resistance movements in German-occupied territories.

Unlike most major powers, the United States entered World War II without a central agency responsible for collecting and disseminating intelligence reports or for coordinating espionage. In fact the confusion at Pearl Harbor was caused in part by the absence of a central clearinghouse for intelligence information. Soon afterward, President Roosevelt established the Office of Strategic Services (OSS) and appointed Colonel William J. Donovan, a lawyer, as director. The OSS became the nation's first official intelligence agency. In addition to enlisting its own operatives and sources of information in the United States and elsewhere, the OSS also organized the intelligence activities of scores of other federal agencies and the armed services.

One of the more significant extensions of federal authority was in the field of science. Although the national government had encouraged various forms of scientific endeavors over the years, it had not undertaken a comprehensive program. War urgencies led Roosevelt to organize a unified national effort. In June 1940, in the midst of the rearmament effort, the president yielded to the pleas of leading scientists to create the National Defense Research Committee, which matched government needs with available scientific resources. A year later Roosevelt established the Office of Scientific Research and Development (OSRD), endowed with direct authority to sponsor scientific research useful to the national security. He chose Vannevar Bush, a leading scientist who had served as president of Johns Hopkins University, as its director. By coordinating scientists and scientific projects, and by initiating new inquiries, the OSRD made many significant contributions. Among its most brilliant breakthroughs was the development of radar and sonar devices which proved essential in the victory over Nazi submarines in the Atlantic and in aerial warfare. Invention of the proximity fuse, a miniature radio set in a shell that detonated it by proximity to a target, ushered in the age of guided missiles. The OSRD also made great advances in the development of blood plasma, which greatly reduced battlefield casualties. In World War I, nine out of ten wounded in combat succumbed to injuries, but in World War II, the ratio was reversed, and only one out of ten died from battle wounds. Great progress was also made in the development of insecticides such as DDT, which eased the burdens of Americans fighting in the Pacific who often found unfamiliar insects almost as deadly as the Japanese.

But the most complicated scientific enterprise sponsored by the OSRD was fabrication of an atomic bomb. Early in 1939 German scientists had accomplished nuclear fission that made it possible to consider eventual production of a powerful bomb. Aware of German advances, scientists in the United States, notably physicists Enrico Fermi and Albert Einstein, persuaded the Administration to sponsor its own atomic program. The OSRD assumed responsibility for this project in 1941. Known as the Manhattan Project, its director, Major-General Leslie Groves, embarked on a far-flung program to coordinate scientific talent. Thousands of scientists in the United States and around the world cooperated in the development of the bomb. Much research was accomplished in Chicago; Berkeley, California;

and at Los Alamos, New Mexico. Plutonium materials for the bomb were manufactured in Oak Ridge, Tennessee, and Hanford, Washington. The vast effort came to fruition in July 1945, when scientists at Los Alamos, working feverishly under the prodding of their director, the brilliant physicist Dr. J. Robert Oppenheimer, finally assembled an atomic bomb. On July 16, 1945, they successfully detonated the first atomic blast in world history at Alamagordo, New Mexico.

Despite intense rivalries and conflicts within the agencies in Washington, they successfully managed the extraordinarily complex problems of national mobilization. Roosevelt's persuasive leadership was the cement that held his disparate administrators and their agencies together while the war experience accelerated the trend toward greater bureaucratic control over many phases of the nation's life. Decision making by individuals was often supplanted by decision making on the part of public agencies. And to sustain themselves, the officials of these agencies often sought to expand their powers and their size.

WAR AND THE ECONOMY

The direction of domestic mobilization gave government a more central role in directing the national economy. World War II saw the development of the military-industrial complex and the subsequent close alliance between government officials and executives of large corporations that accompanied it. Industry executives went to work for the federal government without compensation except a token dollar annually (and became known as "dollar-a-year" men) and federal officials often secured high paying jobs in private industry after leaving government service. The alliance led to a phenomenal production record. Total manufacturing production in 1943 was twice what it had been in the previous year (see Table 1). The individual income of Americans increased correspondingly from $77.6 billion in 1940 to $161.0 billion in 1945 (see Table 2). By 1945 the gross national product had risen from $60 billion in 1940 to $170 billion in 1945. And the national debt skyrocketed (see Table 3). At the end of the war

Table 1
U.S. Aircraft Production

YEAR	AIRCRAFT PRODUCTION
1940	3,807
1941	19,433
1942	47,836
1943	85,898
1944	96,318
1945	46,001

Source: Wesley Frank Craven, James Lea Cate, et al. (eds.), The Army Air Forces In World War II (7 vols., Chicago, 1955), vol. 6, p. 352.

most Americans felt that the Depression—which the New Deal had been unable to shake off—seemed like a bad dream.

The war hastened further concentration of American industry. Fifty-six of the largest companies in the United States received three-fourths of all the federal war contracts. The ten biggest ones garnered almost one-third of the $175 billion awarded in war contracts. To a considerable degree, technological and economic necessity dictated

Table 2
Total National Income, 1939–1945

YEAR	TOTAL NATIONAL INCOME (IN BILLIONS OF DOLLARS)
1939	$ 70.8
1940	77.6
1941	96.9
1942	122.2
1943	149.4
1944	160.7
1945	161.0

Source: Historical Statistics of the U.S.

Table 3
National Debt, 1939–1945

YEAR	NATIONAL DEBT (IN BILLIONS OF DOLLARS)
1939	$ 42.9
1940	42.9
1941	48.9
1942	72.4
1943	136.6
1944	201.0
1945	258.6

Source: Historical Statistics of the U.S.

these choices, for planes, tanks, and guns could not be fabricated effectively by small companies; rather, huge plants employing thousands of workers on assembly lines seemed more efficient for such production.

Aviation and automobile manufacturers built more than 300,000 airplanes, 88,140 tanks, and 3,000 merchant ships. Some increased their output significantly; that was the case with aluminum production. Before 1940 the Aluminum Company of America had held a virtual monopoly on their product. Increasing war demands, however, made its total production so painfully inadequate that Roosevelt ordered a crash program to increase production. Congress authorized more than $300 million for construction of new plants in the Columbia River Valley of the Pacific Northwest, where the Bonneville and Grand Coulee federal power projects would furnish cheap electricity. Other plants were built near the Tennessee Valley Authority, operated by the Aluminum Corporation of America and new competitors like Reynolds or Kaiser Aluminum Company.

Production increases were also achieved when thousands of businesses shifted from civilian to war manufactures. A canning company shifted to the fabrication of parts for merchant ships; a manufacturer of mechanical pencils made bomb parts; a bedding manufacturer turned to mosquito nets; a soft drink bottler loaded shells with explosives. As manufacturers suspended the manufacture of civilian goods, they were able to boost production of war-time products in a relatively short period.

Although the government's share of the nation's capital goods rarely had exceeded 10 percent during the first four decades of the twentieth century, between 1941 and 1945 this proportion doubled, largely because the Roosevelt Administration used public funds to build and equip new manufacturing plants in the United States. After the war many large corporations were allowed to purchase these facilities for a fraction of their original cost.

Of the new, major industries stimulated by the war, synthetic rubber was prominent. When the Japanese captured the Dutch East Indies in 1941, they cut off a major source of America's supply of natural rubber. In this emergency President Roosevelt ordered a crash program to produce a synthetic substitute. Through funds granted by the Reconstruction Finance Corporation, the federal government poured more than $400 million into the construction of new facilities. By 1944 factories produced more than 800,000 tons of synthetic rubber, making the United States virtually self-sufficient for most of its civilian as well as military needs for this product.

The war fostered more efficient organization of industry, and its use of new techniques. A striking illustration was the career of Henry J. Kaiser, a former contractor and builder who in 1941 was attracted to the shipbuilding industry. Scoffing at the methods of the older companies in the industry, Kaiser introduced mass production methods with revolutionary results. In 1940 it took Todd Shipyards more than three hundred days to produce a single merchant vessel; in 1942 Kaiser reduced that time to eighty days; and by 1944 his yards set a record by completing a 10,000 ton liberty ship in just seventeen days. Kaiser achieved his remarkable records by using prefabricated materials, close coordination of diverse processes, and by motivating his workers with high pay and attractive fringe benefits.

The harnessing of the nation's labor power to war-time needs strengthened the role of organizations such as labor unions. After 1939 the booming war industries drew upon the pool of unemployed left by the Depression, and American workers enjoyed rising wages despite federal efforts to freeze salaries for the first time in a decade. By 1942 the once-elusive goal of full employment had been reached. At the end of the war, more than 53 million were employed, including teenagers, women, the aged, and minorities previously excluded by discrimination. At the same time the number of workers organized in unions also rose appreciably, from 7 million to 15 million members. Amid a general cooperative spirit in the nation, less than 1 percent of working time was lost due to strikes. The American worker, not unlike the businessman and the farmer, found that large organizations had become vital instruments for achieving the twin goals of economic security and employment.

Federal financial policies did much to stimulate the phenomenal economic expansion that characterized the American war effort. Federal agencies subsidized the efforts of millions of employers and their employees engaged in the war effort. Altogether, the Treasury pumped $320 billion into the economy, thus lifting the nation out of the Depression and into a new era of prosperity and full employment. At the same time these expenditures led federal officials to make their methods of tax collection more efficient. An excess-profits tax, whereby extraordinarily high profits reverted to the Treasury, was instituted on business. To avoid a possible postwar depression, though, federal regulations permitted companies to claim refunds on war-time tax payments to cover possible losses in the future. Another innovation was the payroll deduction; by withholding taxes at the source, the Internal Revenue Service increased efficiency and lowered collection costs. Through tax policies, as well as through mandatory ceiling prices imposed by the Office of Price Administration, the federal government was able to contain the usual war-time inflation successfully. During the war years the rate of price increases did not exceed an average rate of five percent annually.

What the war experience revealed to the American people was that the federal government, if necessary, could effectively manage the economy. It could stimulate production, facilitate full employment, create a higher standard of living, and still keep the nation solvent. That role, many Americans felt, should be continued after the war, lest the nation once again sink into depression and mass unemployment.

Many Americans realized that full employment and prosperity were due largely to extensive federal expenditures related to the war effort.

This seemed to provide evidence that many proponents of Keynesian economic theories needed to persuade their doubters. Lord John Maynard Keynes, the British economist, advocated deficit spending by governments in time of depression, and manipulation of taxes and interest rates to generate economic prosperity. The solution to depression and unemployment seemed at hand. Did the war not prove the theory? Such a belief buoyed Democrats as well as Republicans, and led government at every level to hire professional economists whose influence on public policy became greater than in previous periods. Indeed, during the war and in the three decades thereafter economists played an increasingly important role in American society.

Agriculture also rose to the challenge. Farmers increased their production by almost one-third, providing food not only for domestic consumption and the nation's armed forces but for American allies, especially England and the Soviet Union. Their achievement was especially remarkable in view of the fact that the number of farmers had declined by 17 percent between 1940 and 1945 as they went to cities to take advantage of lucrative jobs in industry. Moreover, farm labor was woefully inadequate. If high production quotas were met by farmers, it was due not only to increased individual effort, but also to increasing mechanization. The use of a machine such as the mechanical cotton picker and of new chemicals and insecticides reduced manpower needs. The sizes of farms also increased as larger units absorbed smaller or less efficient operations.

America's phenomenal production record in manufacturing, farming, and labor was admired throughout the world. It made Americans aware of the enormous potential in human and material resources that had gone unused during the bitter years of the Depression. The experience strengthened the faith of millions of Americans in big business as an institution. They came to perceive, rightly or wrongly, that full employment and maximum production somehow were closely related to increased government activity of an economy in which large corporations played a major role. The federal government could, the World War II experience revealed, provide needed investment capital and regulate levels of consumer demand so as to maintain full employment. In this manner the faith of millions of Americans in the role of large organizations such as big government, corporations, agriculture, and labor unions in dealing with the nation's major problems was strengthened. Americans thus entered the post-war era with a positive if somewhat naive belief in the efficacy of an organizational society.

POLITICS IN WARTIME

The war did not lead to a suspension of political activities. After Pearl Harbor the national chairmen of the Democratic and the Republican parties announced that they would keep politics out of the war, but political processes continued to operate. Opponents of the New Deal feared that the president would expand reforms under the guise of war-time necessity, and supporters of the president often appealed to patriotism in order to gain political advantages. The number of voters declined during the war, in part because persons in the armed forces sometimes found it difficult to obtain absentee ballots, and highly paid war workers were disinclined to take time off to vote. Then, too, since so many Americans moved about and changed their residences, they often did not meet minimum resident requirements for voting in localities and states.

The trend toward conservatism that had begun as a reaction to the New Deal continued to gather strength during the war. Many New Deal policies were suspended in the heat of war, in part because of the pressures of a conservative coalition in Congress composed of Southern Democrats and Republicans. This coalition began to gather strength in 1938 and continued to attract followers during the war. In the congressional elections of 1942, the Republicans won 209 seats in the House, just a few less than the majority of 218. Essentially, the conservatives opposed the increasingly centralized and government-dominated society, which, New Dealers argued, was necessary to cope with crises such as depressions and wars. Conservatives winced at price controls, rationing, and increased federal regulations, and they opposed expansion of Social Security, public housing programs, or federal health insurance. Still, the coalition was hesitant to repeal the bulk of New Deal legislation, and indeed, in the presidential election of 1944, Republican candidate Governor Thomas E. Dewey of New York promised to retain the New Deal, but pledged himself to administer it more effectively.

Many leaders of American business held key positions in administrative agencies and were in a position to affect public policies significantly. Congress had suspended the antitrust laws, exempted insurance companies from federal regulation, and framed tax laws that were especially attractive to Big Business. Temporary New Deal programs that restricted business, such as the PWA, WPA, CCC, NYA, and the National Resources and Planning Board, were ended.

The activities of labor unions were restricted, in part due to the activities of the new coalition. The Connally-Smith Act gave the president power to seize factories or mines, prohibited strike activity by union leaders in plants seized by the federal government, and forbade political contributions by labor unions. Critics of labor also had a greater voice than during peaceful times. Even the Administration opposed across-the-board wage increases, fearing their inflationary impact. Still, Roosevelt's proposal to limit salaries at the upper levels to $25,000 yearly met steely opposition in Congress.

The congressional coalition did not act in the field of civil rights, except to oppose the repeal of poll taxes.

The war introduced new issues into politics—issues dealing with mobilization, military strategy, and foreign affairs. Thus, it weakened the consensus of the urban coalition that had been the backbone of the New Deal. Roosevelt conceded, "The weaknesses and many of the social inequalities as of 1932 have been repaired or removed, and the job now is, first and foremost, to win the war."

The new conservative coalition was active not only in Congress but in the federal bureaucracy as well. Many of the New Deal lawyers, social workers, and economists who had come to Washington to staff federal agencies during the New Deal departed. Some retired, some went with the waning of reform, and some were forced out by political opponents. In their place came conservative lawyers, businessmen, and engineers and technicians. As the influence of Edward R. Stettinius, James V. Forrestal, and Henry L. Stimson increased, that of individuals such as Henry A. Wallace, Rexford Tugwell, and Aubrey Williams declined. In the Depression, the public image of business and businessmen had been distinctly unfavorable, but in the heat of war, businessmen occupied vital positions of power in the mobilization program, and their prestige grew enormously. The business executive once again became one of the nation's heroes.

Although the issue was rarely mentioned in campaign rhetoric, the war inexorably speeded up regimentation of American life that had begun to accelerate under the New Deal. To many Americans it seemed that the manifold problems of a complex technological society required specialized experts and rigorous organization. War-time exigencies greatly expanded the power and influence of bureaucracy. All this seemed necessary and even good, yet many Americans grew to resent the growth of government influence, even though they felt helpless to stem its tide. Some of these feelings of frustration were reflected by Congressman Martin Dies, chairman of the House Un-American Activities Committee, in 1943 when he asked his colleagues to "guard jealously and zealously the rights and prerogatives of this body [lest] the real power and function of government will not be exercised in this chamber, but . . . by bureaucracy." Another manifestation of these feelings was the establishment of a Special Investigative Committee into the War Program chaired by Senator Harry S. Truman of Missouri. Beginning in 1941, the Truman Committee investigated most phases of the mobilization program, ferreting out waste, inefficiency, and corruption. One of its prime aims was to supervise the reorganization of American society as it girded for total war. The committee proved to be invaluable, and saved taxpayers millions. It was praised by both Democrats as well as Republicans and made Senator Truman a nationally known political figure.

As the presidential election of 1944 approached, speculation concerning Roosevelt understandably increased, but Roosevelt remained silent concerning his intentions. Only a week before the meeting of the Democratic convention, however, he announced that he would accept a nomination for a fourth term if it were offered. "All that is within me cries out to go back to my home on the Hudson River," he said. "But as a good soldier . . . I will accept and serve." Although the convention was ready to nominate him for a fourth term, the party's professionals resolutely opposed the renomination of Henry A. Wallace as vice-president. Most considered him impractical and too radical. After considerable negotiations Truman was chosen to be the president's running mate in 1944. The party platform pledged continuation of the New Deal and international cooperation.

Among the Republicans, Dewey was an early favorite. Willkie had lost the support of party leaders, in part because of his public approval of many of Roosevelt's policies. Dewey easily won the Republican nomination on the first ballot, and he chose Governor John W. Bricker of Ohio as vice-presidential candidate. The platform proposed no major changes in domestic or foreign policies.

The campaign was a contest of personalities more than issues. Rumors that Roosevelt's health was failing persisted, although he made strenuous campaign tours throughout the nation. The rigors of electioneering did, in fact, tax the president's strength. Roosevelt was elected to an unprecedented fourth term. The final returns showed over 25 million votes for Roosevelt and 22 million for Dewey. Americans appeared reluctant to change leaders in the final phases of the war. The election seemed to reveal broad consensus on domestic and foreign policies, and the increased political strength of urban areas. This consensus and the mood of the nation were the result of the war.

As few other events in the lives of most Americans would do, the Second World War greatly accelerated the growth of an organizational society in the United States, a society whose destinies were increasingly determined by government, large corporations, and big organizations rather than by individuals. Unease over these developments was only beginning to surface in the thoughts of most Americans, and would not become an issue for many years.

CHAPTER 12

Social and Cultural Impact of World War II

Without question the Second World War wrought significant changes in American society and culture, changes that created the affluent society of the post-war decade. One of the more obvious effects of the war mobilization was to increase the mobility of people, and as a result, to accelerate the pace of urbanization. When individuals or families moved about, often to new or unfamiliar places, unwittingly they brought important social changes into their lives. In the process of moving, families tended to be disrupted, women entered the labor force in increasing numbers, and youths and children were often left to shift for themselves. The disintegration of family and friendship ties led to a greater demand for social services by governments in such areas as housing, health, and education.

The war had an even greater impact on minorities, who were quick to sense that government programs in war-time could help them to achieve many of their goals, particularly the attainment of equality. The war opened up new job opportunities for minorities, and in addition federal regulations requiring fair employment practices reduced discrimination. Service in the armed forces often opened the door to vocational training, travel, education, and other benefits. Minority-group concentration in the cities led to stronger political representation by minorities and a new sense of political power. And the concentration of blacks, Mexican-Americans, and other minorities in cities like New York, Detroit, Chicago, and Los Angeles gave them a heightened sense of cultural identity.

THE NEW MOBILITY

The new mobility was probably a major factor in changing values. More than 12 million men and women served in the armed forces. They traveled extensively, not only within the United States but throughout the world. At the same time families at home were also frequently uprooted. Sometimes wives of servicemen followed them, or they went to live with families or friends. More than 15 million civilians moved about in search of new economic opportunities, often traveling to secure lucrative war jobs. Since industries were usually located in urban areas, their populations swelled considerably. Such movement left its mark on people who came in contact with new environments and with strangers. Americans became more cosmopolitan and developed a broader, more tolerant outlook as a result of their extensive travels.

Extensive mobility also led many persons to feel alienated or uprooted. Urban crowding and congestion or competition for jobs created many tensions which sometimes found an outlet in violence.

Housing became tight as a result of the war and the great mobility. Tent cities and automobile trailer camps became common sights wherever war plants were located. Not far from Detroit, for example, the Ford Motor Company constructed its giant Willow Run factory to build bombers. Before 1941 fewer than 15,000 persons lived in the area, but as Willow Run moved to full-scale production, an additional 32,000 workers moved there. Their makeshift camps aroused the ire of older residents and created genuine fire safety and sanitation hazards. Public transportation systems in most localities were usually ill-equipped to handle such large numbers. The sudden increase of people in an area placed enormous strains on social services, schools, hospitals, churches, and indeed, most local institutions. Under such pressures houses and other living accommodations rapidly deteriorated. In fact, many of the problems associated with urban blight in the post-war decades had their origins in the mass migration to urban areas during World War II.

Once families moved to cities, they were often subject to disintegrative influences. If fathers were not away in the armed forces, they were likely to work long hours in various types of war work. Mothers were just as likely to be away from home, because mobilization created new job opportunities for women, and increasing numbers entered the labor force. The labor shortage also created opportunities for older or retired individuals as well as for teen-agers.

The family as a social unit was placed under great strains. The disruption of families created psychological tensions among adults, which were reflected in higher rates of divorce, mental illness, and violence. These tensions were also reflected in the increase of juvenile delinquency.

NEW ROLES FOR WOMEN

The war probably altered the role of women more than any other segment of the population. With men away in the armed forces—or engaged in demanding occupations—millions of women became the effective heads of families. In a sense many families became matriarchal. No less striking was the increase in the number of working women. The number of females who took jobs rose from 12 million in 1941 to 16.5 million in 1945. Many were in occupations once considered exclusively the domain of males such as locomotive oilers or welders. During the war many women worked on assembly lines, and others could be found in steel plants around blast furnaces or rolling mills. For the first time in an American war, women were permitted to join the armed forces as other than nurses. In the Women's Army Corps (WACs), Women's Auxiliary Naval Service (WAVES), and in the Marines, women performed varied duties as officers or enlisted personnel which freed men for combat service. Many women left their war-time jobs in 1945 to become home-makers. Still, the percentage of females in the labor force in 1950 was larger than in 1940, reflecting a steady increase in the number of America's working women.

The large numbers of women who went outside the home to work was bound to affect the rearing of children. The physical absence of a mother who worked or who was preoccupied with the pressures of her work invariably influenced children who sometimes felt neglected, or who became tense and anxious. Psychiatrists debated the emotional effects of a mother's absence from her children. Some social workers and educators saw a partial solution to the problem in the establishment of day care centers and nursery schools. Such institutions mushroomed during the war as they took over child-rearing responsibilities, once traditionally the responsibility of the family. Under the Lanham Act (1940), the federal government built 2,800 child care centers, and these were but a small fraction of those established for pre-school children.

Others saw a connection between working mothers and a statistical rise in juvenile delinquency. Crimes for persons under 18 shot up five-fold during the war years.

CHANGES IN EDUCATION

In many parts of the nation, schools were overcrowded and under-staffed. Children in congested industrial areas often attended school for only half a day. Some schools, particularly elementary schools in rural areas, were left without teachers. The proliferation of well-paying jobs tempted many youngsters to leave school to enter the labor force. The number of working teen-agers rose from 1 to 3 million between 1940 and 1944, and more than 1 million dropped out of school to go to work. Even young children between the ages of seven and twelve worked part-time—as delivery or errand runners, pinsetters in bowling alleys, or doing general work in retail stores.

The nation's high schools sought to meet war-time demands and to counteract the drop-out problem by broadening their curriculums to include new language courses, world history, and additional vocational training programs in war-related skills such as welding or aircraft mechanics. Some schools attempted to solve the drop-out problem by offering late afternoon or evening classes. Meanwhile, the armed forces denuded colleges of students as well as faculty. Most institutions maintained only a fraction of their pre-war enrollments and many enrolled mostly women. The precarious existence of colleges led the army and navy to use them for special training programs for service personnel. The army's Specialized Training Program stressed language skills, social sciences, and humanities, and was similar to the Navy's V12 program.

Exposure to higher education and the world whetted the desire of many Americans who had been unable to afford advanced education before the war. Such desires were enough to persuade Congress to enact the GI Bill of Rights in June 1944. Every ex-service person was entitled to paid education or training at any level for one year, plus the time spent in the armed forces up to four years. The bill also authorized unemployment payments for veterans, job referral services, medical care, pensions, and re-employment rights. It gave "emphatic notice to the men and women in the armed forces," Roosevelt said, "that the American people do not intend to let them down." Congress also hoped that the GI Bill would help to prevent another depression after the war, caused by the mustering out of more than 10 million members of the armed forces and the inevitable slowing down of the post-war economy. The GI Bill, together with the various federal programs in education, would transform the nation's colleges and universities into centers for national scientific research and vocational instruction after the war.

THE WAR AND THE GROWTH OF MASS MEDIA

The war also spurred tendencies toward a more formal organization of American culture, particularly in the mass media. The publishing industry was propelled toward a greater emphasis on mass production by the needs of the armed forces for vast quantities of inexpensive reading materials. To relieve boredom of American military personnel stationed in remote areas, the United States Government Printing Office published the Armed Services Editions, reprints of thousands of books in a paperback format. These books rolled off the presses in large numbers—more than 350 million—and did much to introduce Americans to paperback books. Armed forces publications such as *Stars and Stripes* or the army humor magazine *Yank* gave experience in publishing mass circulation magazines to many men who went on to become stars of post-war journalism such as Bill Mauldin. Propaganda—whether in war films such as *Guadalcanal Diary* and *Wake Island* or in radio broadcasts beamed by the Office of War Information provided experience for thousands of individuals who entered the advertising industry after the war and helped to develop the advertising boom in the affluent society of the 1950s.

Hollywood made an all-out effort to turn its talents to the war effort. Skilled screenwriters composed scripts to meet the specifications of the Office of War Information, while famous directors of the caliber of Frank Capra devoted much of their time to war-oriented or propagandistic films. If the war did not actually inaugurate new developments in American culture, it did much to accelerate the trend toward an increasingly centralized and powerful mass media.

MINORITIES DURING THE WAR

Attracted by new economic opportunities, members of minority groups abandoned rural areas and migrated in droves to towns and cities. Black tenant farmers and field workers from the South, Mexican-American migrant farm workers, and Native-Americans flocked to factories. Once in an urban environment, they faced many new and unfamiliar problems. They competed with other groups for scarce housing, social services, and often confronted overt or subtle discrimination. Despite the difficulties, most minorities found new opportunities in urban life, which they hoped would improve their status in American society.

Among the newcomers to the cities, black Americans were prominent. Drawn by the lure of well-paying factory jobs in the Midwest and the West, large numbers of rural blacks from the South migrated. They streamed to industrial cities such as Cleveland, Detroit, and Chicago. For the first time also many blacks settled on the Pacific Coast, where shipyards and aircraft factories needed labor sorely. The shortage of workers broke down many of the racial barriers that had prevented blacks from finding jobs in industry. Altogether, perhaps as many as 1 million southern blacks moved to other regions during the war. The number of black war workers increased from 3 percent of the labor force in 1942 to 8 percent in 1945. The number of skilled black workers doubled.

As black Americans were uprooted by and contributed to the war effort, they sought more aggressively to diminish racial discrimination. Availability of war jobs also provided blacks with greater economic power than they had known before. Concentration of blacks in cities gave them a greater sense of political power, and more than 800,000 blacks served in the armed forces, which, while still segregated, opened up new hopes for social equality. Overseas assignments led many blacks to experience a new sense of dignity. Moreover, the contrast between the war-time emphasis on brotherhood and equality in democratic societies as distinguished from the rampant racism of Germany served as an embarrassing reminder to Americans of the racial prejudices in their own society.

The war also hastened the organization of blacks into more well-defined protest groups, which could press their demands more effectively. Between 1941 and 1945 black Americans became increasingly more militant in their advocacy of civil rights. There was a March on Washington Movement, founded by J. Philip Randolph in the summer of 1941. Randolph, president of the Brotherhood of Sleeping Car Porters, believed that massive protest rather than acquiescence would win blacks greater rights. As early as May 1941 he called upon blacks to undertake "a thundering march . . . to shake up white America." Randolph hoped to mobilize the black man on the street and black tenant farmers rather than the black elite. Because he advocated direct action rather than traditional methods such as court battles, the black press tended to be cool to his calls for action. President Roosevelt did not look favorably upon the movement, for he feared that it would disrupt national unity and heighten racial tensions. Randolph agreed to cancel the protest march on Washington, which threatened to embarrass the Administration, if the president would create a Fair Employment Practices Commission. This directive, issued by executive order, instructed all federal agencies and federal defense contractors to end discrimination in hiring. (It did not, however, affect the armed forces.) To enforce this new policy, a Fair Employment Practices Commission, which could hear complaints from aggrieved individuals or groups, was created. Although the agency lacked statutory authority, it effectively used the threat of withholding government contracts to break down discriminatory barriers against black workers. Greatly encouraged, during 1942 Randolph called upon blacks to engage in mass marches on city halls to demand civil rights. His call went largely unheeded, as an increasingly large number of blacks found well-paying jobs in the booming war economy. In 1943 Randolph urged blacks to engage in civil disobedience to protest Jim Crow practices in the South and in the North. This was also the year of race riots in Detroit and New York City, and blacks as well as whites were fearful of further domestic violence.

A recognition that organization could heighten the effectiveness of black protests also underlay the formation of the Congress of Racial Equality in 1942. The organization was inspired by the theories of nonviolent resistance developed by India's great leader, Mahatma Gandhi. As early as 1943 CORE sponsored sit-ins to integrate restaurants and movie theaters in major cities.

The NAACP and the Urban League continued to be the most important black organizations to espouse civil rights. Due to the increasing prosperity and interest in racial equality, the NAACP was able to quadruple its membership between 1941 and 1945. This growth gave its leaders confidence that they could influence national politics and legislation to attain their goal of racial equality. Yet, they sensed that winning the war superseded civil rights for the time being, and although the NAACP and Urban League continued to advocate the achievement of racial justice via judicial action and publicity, they kept their demands more muted than the proposed March on Washington or CORE sit-in activity.

Even so, the strivings of black Americans often created tensions that erupted into violence.

Few cities were more directly affected than was Detroit, Michigan. More than 500,000 people had come between 1940 and 1943 to take advantage of the thousands of newly created war jobs. At least 60,000 blacks were living in some of the worst housing in the nation. Local ethnic groups, including Poles and Irish, resented the newcomers, who they felt were causing rapid deterioration of the central city. Only a spark was needed to ignite hostile feelings, and that spark occurred on a hot, muggy Sunday evening, June 23, 1943. A group of teenagers—black and white—began a melee in a recreation park located near Paradise Valley, a predominantly black neighborhood. As rumors of rape, assault, and murder spread through black and white sections of the city, thousands of Detroiters poured into the streets bound for vengeance. Blacks attacked unsuspecting white workers just returning from the night shift or white motorists and pedestrians near black neighborhoods. Bands of whites attacked innocent black passengers on streetcars and buses. The Detroit police attempted to control looters and rooftop snipers in the black ghetto, with limited success. The next day the situation became even more menacing. When a large and angry crowd of whites milled around the edge of Paradise Valley, a frightened black began to shoot at them indiscriminately. Within hours thousands of rioters roamed the streets of the black neighborhood, looting, burning, and inflicting violence. When it became obvious that the police were unable to subdue the rioters, federal assistance was requested. Six thousand National Guardsmen arrived in Detroit on Monday evening. They patrolled streets, and by the end of the week, order had been restored. Twenty-five blacks and nine whites lost their lives in the Detroit riot, and nearly one thousand individuals were injured.

Other cities also throbbed with tensions. Although the Harlem Riot of 1943 in New York City was not as destructive as the Detroit riot, it reflected the same kind of racial antagonisms. It began on August 1, 1943, with an inaccurate rumor that a white policeman had killed a black serviceman. Thousands of blacks rampaged along 125th Street, Harlem's main thoroughfare. The New York police deputized 1,500 blacks to help restore order. Perhaps because many Harlem residents were unsympathetic to the rioters, their effective self-policing quickly contained the disturbances, but not before 6 blacks were killed and more than 300 were injured.

The winds of change which the war set into motion also reached into the communities of Native-Americans. Since they were a rural people living in remote areas, the international crisis seemed very distant. Yet a sufficient number sensed a threat to their own independence if the Axis powers won. Thus, Native-Americans responded generously to the war effort. The Crow tribe in Montana, for example, offered all its resources to the government. In Santa Ana, New Mexico, Pueblo Indians went to their ancient shrine on December 8, 1941, and remained in prayer for one month. The Zuni Pueblo, although desperately poor, donated generously to Red Cross war appeals. The Indians of the Six Nations of the Iroquois Confederacy, in New York, as an independent nation even declared war on the Axis.

In addition, many Native-Americans actively participated in the war effort. More than 29,000 Native-Americans served in the armed forces. A contingent of Navajos formed a special services unit in the Army's Signal Corps, where they used their language for secret communications that completely confounded the Germans. In the Pacific, the Marines also organized a similar special unit of Navajos. Approximately one hundred thousand Indians migrated to cities to take war jobs. Most Indians remained on reservations, however, but took advantage of jobs in their localities that became available because of a general labor shortage. More than two thousand Navajos, for example, worked on the construction of the Fort Wingate Ordnance Depot near Gallup, New Mexico.

In various ways the war accelerated the culture shock that Native-Americans were forced to cope with. Those Native-Americans who served in the armed forces, which were integrated with regard to them, felt at loose ends at the completion of their service—unsure whether to return to their traditional ways or to adapt to the white culture. Those who held war jobs found adjustment to urban living extremely difficult and were keenly conscious of their lack of skills or education. And many Native-Americans who stayed on their lands, where they were desperately poor, suffered from the suspension of many federal and New Deal programs as the government assigned priority to winning of the war to all other aims. The war threatened whatever progress had been made during the New Deal in achieving greater self-determination and sharpened the cultural conflict between mainstream American and Native-American values.

Spanish-speaking Americans were influenced by war-time experiences in many ways. Most lived in the Southwest and the West, and significant numbers could be found also in barrios of midwestern cities. Small farmers living in southern Colorado and northern New Mexico eked out a meager living on lands that they had occupied for many generations. In most areas Mexican-Americans were poor unskilled or semi-skilled workers with little education, subject to ethnic discrimination. The availability of new jobs in the war economy opened new vistas for Spanish-speaking Americans. In the rural villages of New Mexico, for example, one-half of the male population left to secure work in larger towns and cities. Many learned new trades under the auspices of the State Department of Vocational Education. Others secured jobs in industries which had not previously afforded them opportunities.

The Mexican-American response to the war effort was enthusiastic. Often isolated in small villages or urban barrios, Mexican-Americans found military service a bridge to the outside world from which they had largely been excluded. Throughout the nation Mexican-Americans volunteered for the armed forces in numbers much higher than warranted by their proportion in the population. New Mexico—with its large Spanish-speaking population—had the largest number of military volunteers per capita of any state in the nation. Many New Mexicans served in the Philippines in the 200th and 515th Coast Artillery. Seventeen Mexican-Americans earned the Congressional Medal of Honor. Of the fourteen Texans who were awarded the medal, five were Mexican-American.

Among the war heroes of the Mexican-American community was Guy Gabaldon, who talked 1,000 Japanese into surrendering at the Battle of Saipan. Jose Martinez of Colorado had the distinction of being the first draftee to win the Congressional Medal of Honor.

In the first year of the war, discrimination against Mexican-Americans was widespread, whether in copper mines of Arizona or in the shipyards and oil refineries on the Gulf or Pacific Coasts. But as the labor shortage increased, many of these barriers fell, and Mexican-Americans were able to secure better paying jobs. To relieve the shortage of farm labor, the United States government negotiated an agreement with Mexico, which provided for the import of *braceros,* temporary Mexican field workers, into California, Arizona, and Texas. American employers were to supply transportation and proper housing for these transients, and to pay them according to prevailing wage scales.

In 1942 President Roosevelt appointed Carlos Castaneda of the University of Texas to the dual roles of special assistant on Latin American problems and assistant to the chairman of the Fair Employment Practices Commission. A Spanish-Speaking People's Division was created in the Office of Inter-American Affairs. Under the direction of Carey McWilliams—a well-known writer who championed the cause of Mexican-Americans—this office sought to lessen discrimination against Spanish-speaking Americans. Its influence, for example, led to a lessening of segregation in public schools, particularly in California and Texas. Texas established teacher training institutes during World War II to enable teachers to deal with Spanish-speaking students.

War-generated tensions also affected Mexican-Americans. In Los Angeles groups of Mexican-American youths formed *Pachuco* gangs, known for their distinctive attire, which consisted of zoot suits—a flashy suit with flared knee trousers—long hair, broad-rimmed felt hats, and pocket knives. These gangs roamed the streets and engaged in acts of vandalism, sometimes attacking servicemen from nearby bases. Frequently rival gangs fought. In June of 1943 a group of sailors from the Chavez Ravine Naval Base roamed the east Los Angeles section where the gangs were concentrated. Without much police interference, they attacked the gangs as well as any blacks who were in sight. A large-scale riot involving more than one thousand youths ensued, lasting two days before order could be restored. During the spring of 1943 similar smaller disturbances rocked San Diego, Long Beach, Chicago, Detroit, and Philadelphia.

JAPANESE-AMERICANS DURING THE WAR

Of all the victims of discrimination, the Japanese-Americans were treated to the most extreme form of racial prejudice. It is true that the treatment of aliens by the federal government in the Second World War contrasted favorably with World War I experience. In 1919–1920 aliens had been harrassed and imprisoned—and the federal government freely violated their civil rights. By contrast, from 1941 to 1945 the federal courts zealously guarded the civil liberties of aliens or opponents of the war. But Japanese, and Japanese-Americans of Japanese ancestry (Nisei) were an exception.

Soon after Pearl Harbor Secretary of War Henry L. Stimson and the War Department urged President Roosevelt to remove about 120,000 Japanese—aliens as well as citizens—from the West Coast, where most of them resided. In part they were responding to the clamor of important public figures on the Pacific Coast such as California's Attorney General Earl Warren, who later became a Supreme Court justice. Some westerners feared collaboration if there were a direct attack by Japanese naval forces. Others had disliked the Japanese-Americans for decades, resenting their lack of assimilation and their skills in farming, horticulture, and commerce. Pearl Harbor crystallized many of these fears and prejudices. "We believe that when we are dealing with the Caucasian race, we have methods that will test the loyalty of them," declared Earl Warren, "but when we deal with the Japanese, we are in an entirely different field, and we cannot form any opinion that we believe to be sound." As such pressures converged on the White House, in March 1942 President Roosevelt requested congressional authorization to order the evacuation of all Japanese-Americans from the Pacific Coast.

By June the federal government had herded more than one hundred thousand Japanese-Americans into hastily erected detention camps in seven western states in the Rocky Mountain region. Most evacuees were allowed to bring only a few personal items and clothing. They were forced to abandon their homes, their businesses, and all other possessions. In the camps—administered by the War Relocation Authority—Japanese-Americans lived in large, wooden barracks furnished with army cots. They were provided with communal eating and recreational facilities. Many of the persons detained were bitter, for they were loyal Americans who had committed no offense. Their racial ancestry was the sole reason for their internment. Some sought legal recourse. In *Hirabayashi* v. *U.S.* the Supreme Court upheld the right of military officials to detain Japanese and Japanese-Americans. In December 1944, however, the court noted in *ex parte Endo* that detention of loyal persons was illegal. As the wave of war hysteria subsided in 1943, the War Relocation Authority began a program of gradual release. In January 1945 all of the Japanese-Americans still interned were allowed to leave. The experience left deep emotional scars among those who underwent this traumatic experience and was yet another example of the deep-seated racial feelings felt by many Americans.

President Roosevelt did not live to see victory over Japan. Worn down by his grueling pace as commander in chief, by the 1944 election, and the Yalta Conference, he sought rest in late March at one of his favorite vacation retreats in Warm Springs, Georgia. There, on April 12, 1945, while sitting for a portrait, he suddenly collapsed, struck with heart failure. He died within two hours. The entire nation and much of the world mourned his passing, knowing that an epoch in the American experience had come to an end.

Vice President Harry S. Truman continued to press the war against Japan. American air raids on Japan intensified in the spring and summer of 1945. Although rumors of Japanese desires to end the fighting reached Washington, D.C., no substantial settlement had crystallized by July 1945 when Truman met with Churchill and Stalin at Potsdam, Germany, to discuss joint policies. On that occasion the new president warned Japan to surrender. His demand, however, did not elicit an immediate response from the Japanese. Truman made this warning with the knowledge that American scientists had just developed the first atomic bomb in history. On July 28, 1945, Truman authorized its use, and nine days later an American plane dropped the first atomic bomb on Hiroshima, Japan. Its destructiveness was unprecedented. It leveled most of the city and killed more than eighty thousand persons. Three days later American aircraft dropped another atomic bomb on Nagasaki. At the same time the Soviet Union declared war on Japan. In this desperate situation Japan surrendered unconditionally. On September 2, 1945, known as VJ Day, General Douglas MacArthur received the Japanese delegation on the battleship *Missouri* in Tokyo harbor. The global conflict was now officially at an end. More than 292,000 Americans lost their lives fighting, and 671,000 sustained injuries. In terms of lives as well as material cost, the Second World War was the costliest foreign conflict in the nation's history.

When VJ Day came in 1945 few Americans had yet realized just how dramatically the war had transformed American society and culture. The dislocations caused by war, even more than those of the Depression, greatly accelerated the pace of change in America. Millions of Americans had been displaced from jobs, homes, families, and familiar surroundings, and few returned to their pre-war ways. The war had uprooted and transported Americans into an age of affluence. The mood of Americans in 1945, one of optimism and high expectations for the future, was quite different from the fearful, pessimistic mood of the Depression era.

Bibliography

GENERAL WORKS, 1929–1941

Perhaps the best-written account of the New Deal is the series by Arthur Schlesinger, Jr., *The Age of Roosevelt* (3 vols., Boston, 1957–1960), a highly sympathetic work which, unfinished, does not extend beyond 1936. Volume titles are *The Crisis of the Old Order, The Coming of the New Deal,* and *The Politics of Upheaval.* A shorter, general, one-volume work on the New Deal by William E. Leuchtenburg is *Franklin D. Roosevelt and the New Deal 1932–1940* (New York, 1963), which restricts itself largely to politics on the national and international scene. Students desiring a broad but brief survey will benefit from Dexter Perkins, *The New Age of Franklin D. Roosevelt, 1932–1945* (Chicago, 1957). Edgar E. Robinson, a great admirer of Herbert Hoover, presents an indictment of Roosevelt in *The Roosevelt Leadership, 1933–1945* (Philadelphia, 1955). A stimulating foreign view of the era is by Mario Einaudi, author of *The Roosevelt Revolution* (New York, 1959). One of the most graphic descriptions of Depression conditions as they affected working people is found in Irving Bernstein, *The Lean Years* (Boston, 1960). This may be supplemented by an excellent collection of contemporary sources about life during the economic crisis in David Shannon (ed.), *The Great Depression* (Englewood Cliffs, 1960). The psychological suffering wrought by the

Depression is clearly explained in a fine popular work by Caroline Bird called *The Invisible Scar* (New York, 1966).

FRANKLIN D. ROOSEVELT

There exists a large body of biographical literature about Roosevelt. One of the best one-volume biographies is *Roosevelt, the Lion and the Fox* (New York, 1956) by James M. Burns. Frank Freidel is writing a multi-volumed life of Roosevelt of which *Franklin D. Roosevelt: the Apprenticeship* (Boston, 1952), *Franklin D. Roosevelt: the Ordeal* (Boston, 1955), *Franklin D. Roosevelt: the Triumph* (Boston, 1955) and *Franklin D. Roosevelt: the Interregnum* [1932–1933] (Boston, 1976) have already appeared. Rexford Tugwell, in *The Democratic Roosevelt* (Garden City, 1957), presents a shrewd appraisal by a former close associate and member of the Brains Trust. A charming, warm-hearted remembrance of the president by Secretary of Labor Frances Perkins is entitled *The Roosevelt I Knew* (New York, 1946). For a short anthology of original source writings by and about Roosevelt, see Gerald D. Nash (ed.), *Franklin Delano Roosevelt* (Englewood Cliffs, 1967).

THE HUNDRED DAYS

The Hundred Days is the subject of a reminiscence by Brains Truster Rexford Tugwell in *The Brains Trust* (New York, 1968), while the chief Brains Truster Raymond Moley presents his view of this exciting period in *After Seven Years* (New York, 1939). The president's principal speech writer, Samuel Rosenman, reminisces in *Working With Roosevelt* (New York, 1952). Hugh R. Johnson, Administrator of the NRA, discusses the establishment of that agency in *The Blue Eagle, from Egg to Earth* (Garden City, 1935), while Edwin G. Nourse et al. in *Three Years of the Agricultural Adjustment Act* (Washington,

1937) describes the growth of New Deal farm programs. Van L. Perkins in *Crisis in Agriculture: The Agricultural Adjustment Administration and the New Deal* (Berkeley, 1969) provides a later, and more comprehensive, appraisal. Relief efforts are illuminated by Searle Charles in *Minister of Relief: Harry Hopkins and the Depression* (Syracuse, 1963) and in Paul Douglas's *Social Security in the United States* (New York, 1936).

THE EXPERIMENTAL NEW DEAL

The experimental phase of the New Deal is covered in general works noted earlier and in various more specialized studies. The NRA is analyzed in Everett S. Lyon et al. in *The National Recovery Administration* (Washington, 1935) and by one of its chief officials, Donald R. Richberg, in *The Rainbow* (New York, 1936). Fiscal policies are discussed clearly by Herbert Stein, *The Fiscal Revolution in America* (Chicago, 1969). A stimulating discussion of experimentation in farm policies is by Richard S. Kirkendall, *Social Scientists and Farm Politics in the Age of Roosevelt* (Columbia, Mo., 1966). An excellent survey of labor and labor legislation is by Irving Bernstein, *Turbulent Years: A History of the American Worker, 1933–1941* (Boston, 1970). Experiments with relief can be followed in Donald Howard's book, *The WPA and Federal Relief Policy* (New York, 1943) and in Lewis L. Lorwin's book, *Youth Work Programs* (Washington, 1941).

PROTEST AGAINST THE NEW DEAL

Political reaction against the New Deal is described by Irving Howe and Lewis Coser in *The American Communist Party* (New York, 1957) and by David Shannon in *The Decline of American Communism* (New York, 1959). Donald McCoy, author of *Angry Voices* (Lawrence, 1958), deals with reform-minded, third-party groups. A brilliant depiction of Huey Long is T. Harry Williams, *Huey S. Long* (New York, 1969). Abraham Holtzman in *The Townsend Movement: A Political Study* (Syracuse, 1963) is useful as is Charles J. Tully, *Father Coughlin and the New Deal* (Syracuse, 1965). Charles C. Blackorby, *Prairie Rebel: The Public Life of William Lemke* (Lincoln, 1963) outlines a dissident's view of the Roosevelt policies.

THE REFORM NEW DEAL

The reform phase of the New Deal is brilliantly surveyed in *The Age of Roosevelt* (vol. 3) by Arthur Schlesinger, Jr. It can be followed in briefer form in Broadus Mitchell's *Depression Decade* (New York, 1947). On specialized aspects see David C. Lilienthal, *TVA— Democracy on the March* (New York, 1944) and Roscoe C. Martin (ed.), *TVA: The First Twenty Years* (University, Alab., 1956). Roy Lubove, *The Struggle for Social Security* (Cambridge, 1968) is the best single work on the subject. Paul Conkin, *Tomorrow A New World* (Ithaca, 1959) covers community planning by New Deal agencies. Richard S. Polenberg, *Reorganizing Roosevelt's Government, 1936–1939* (Cambridge, Mass., 1966), is a competent monograph on that topic. The New Deal's efforts to develop health policies are discussed in David S. Hirshfield, *The Last Reform: The Campaign for Compulsory Health Insurance in the United States from 1932–1943* (Cambridge, 1970).

THE NEW DEAL AND MINORITIES

On ethnic Americans Oscar Handlin's *The Americans* provides a general survey. Raymond Wolters, in *Negroes and the Great Depression* (Westport, Conn. 1970), covers selected phases of the subject while Gunnar Myrdal's *An American Dilemma* (New York, 1944) is old but still informative. Donald L. Parman, in *The Navajos and the New Deal* (New Haven, 1976), is one of the best works to deal with a large Indian tribe's experiences during the New Deal. On Spanish-speaking Americans selected portions of Matt S. Meier and Feliciano Rivera's *The Chicanos: A History of Mexican-Americans*

(New York, 1972) provide an overview, as does Manuel Servin (ed.) in *The Mexican-Americans* (Beverly Hills, 1970). Abraham Hoffman, in *Unwanted Mexican-Americans in the Great Depression* (Tucson, 1974), probes one phase of the Chicano experience. As yet no adequate work has appeared to trace the history of women during the New Deal. The brief discussion in this volume is based on contemporary newspaper accounts, including the *New York Times*.

THE NEW DEAL AND CULTURAL LIFE

In recent years much has been written on cultural life during the Great Depression. Daniel Aaron, in *Writers on the Left* (New York, 1961) analyzes one segment of the literary scene, and Maxwell Geismar, *Writers in Crisis* (New York, 1942), and Edmund Wilson, *The Shores of Light* (New Haven, 1952), provide perceptive evaluations by contemporary literary critics. A detailed account of the WPA Writers Project by a former participant is Jerre Mangione's *The Dream and the Deal* (Boston, 1972). William F. McDonald's *Federal Relief Administration and the Arts* (Columbus, 1969) is a comprehensive survey, while *Music in the United States, A Historical Introduction* by H. Wiley Hitchcock (2d. ed., Englewood Cliffs, 1974), offers a succinct and informative summary of the 1930s. Jane D. Mathews's *The Federal Theatre* (Princeton, 1967) is the best work on this experiment.

DIPLOMACY DURING THE DEPRESSION

The diplomacy of the Depression is capably surveyed in Robert Divine in *The Illusion of Neutrality* (Chicago, 1962) and Donald F. Drummond in *The Passing of American Neutrality 1937–1941* (Ann Arbor, 1955). The works of Selig Adler, *The Isolationist Impulse* (London, 1957), and Wayne S. Cole, *America First* (Madison, 1953), deal more specifically with isolationist sentiment. A more specialized and detailed account is by William L. Langer and S. Everett Gleason, *The Challenge to Isolation, 1937–1940* (New York, 1952). Charles A.

Beard, in *American Foreign Policy in the Making, 1932–1940* (New Haven, 1946), offers a severe indictment of the Roosevelt policies.

THE ROAD TO WAR

A fine overall survey of the European and world situation is Gordon Wright's *The Ordeal of Total War, 1939–1945* (New York, 1968). Many of the problems of mobilizing American resources in peacetime are surveyed by Eliot Janeway in *The Struggle for Survival* (2d ed., New Haven, 1968) and Bruce Catton in *The War Lords of Washington* (New York, 1949). Cordell Hull, in *The Memoirs of Cordell Hull* (2 vols., New York, 1948), and Henry Stimson and McGeorge Bundy, in *On Active Service in Peace and War* (New York, 1948), provide a vivid sense of immediacy for these years. A rather detailed account of the worsening international situation is in William L. Langer's and S. E. Gleason's *The Undeclared War, 1940–1941* (New York, 1953). On the election of 1940, Ellsworth Barnard, *Wendell Willkie* (New York, 1966), is useful in recreating the atmosphere. Worsening relations between the United States and Japan can be followed in Herbert Feis's *The Road to Pearl Harbor* (New York, 1950) and in the popular, well-written book by Walter Millis, *This is Pearl Harbor* (New York, 1947). A scholarly analysis is by Paul W. Schroeder, *The Axis Alliance and Japanese American Relations, 1948* (Urbana, 1958). A recollection of Pearl Harbor day is vividly recounted by Walter Lord in *Day of Infamy* (New York, 1957).

ROOSEVELT'S MILITARY AND DIPLOMATIC
POLICIES DURING WORLD WAR II

One of the best books to summarize President Roosevelt's role as commander in chief is James M. Burns, *Roosevelt, The Soldier of Freedom, 1940–1945* (New York, 1970). A leading military analyst, Hanson W. Baldwin, critically appraises Roosevelt's major military decisions in *Great Mistakes of the War* (New York, 1950). Kent R. Greenfield (ed.), in *Command Decisions* (Washington, 1959), offers a more favorable evaluation. A detailed factual summary of United

States military policies is A. Russell Buchanan, *The United States and World War II* (2 vols., New York, 1964). Brief surveys of Roosevelt's war diplomacy include Robert A. Divine, *Roosevelt and World War II* (Baltimore, 1969), and Gaddis Smith, *American Diplomacy During the Second World War* (New York, 1964). The war-time conferences of the Big Three are admirably covered in Herbert Feis's *Churchill, Roosevelt, Stalin: The War They Waged and the Peace They Sought* (New York, 1957). New Left critiques of F.D.R.'s diplomacy include Gabriel Kolko, *The Politics of War* (New York, 1969), and Lloyd C. Gardner, *Architects of Illusion* (New York, 1970).

DOMESTIC MOBILIZATION IN WARTIME

Wartime mobilization is discussed in the works of Eliot Janeway, *The Struggle for Survival* (2d ed., New Haven, 1968), Bruce Catton, *The War Lords of Washington* (New York, 1949), and Richard Polenberg, *War and Society* (Philadelphia, 1972). James P. Baxter III, *Scientists Against Time* (New York, 1946) skillfully summarizes war-time scientific activities. Donald M. Nelson, in *Arsenal for Democracy* (New York, 1948), provides an insider's view. The role of the economy is ably sketched by D. L. Gordon and Royden Dangerfield, in *The Hidden Weapon: The Story of Economic Warfare* (New York, 1947) and by W. W. Wilcox in *The Farmer in the Second World War* (Ames, Iowa, 1947). As yet, a good book on politics during the war still has not been written. Roland Young, *Congressional Politics in the Second World War* (New York, 1956) surveys the legislative scene, while D. R. B. Ross, *Preparing for Ulysses: Politics and Veterans During World War II* (New York, 1969), discusses demobilization problems.

THE SOCIAL AND CULTURAL IMPACT OF WORLD WAR II

Writings about the social and cultural impact of the Second World War are scattered. A broad contemporary survey is Jack Goodman (ed.), *While You Were Gone* (New York, 1946). Richard S. Polenberg, *War and Society* (Philadelphia, 1972), touches on major issues. A popular potpourri is Geoffrey Perrett, *Days of Sadness, Years of Triumph: The American People, 1939–1945* (New York, 1973). Cultural trends are breezily discussed in Russell Lynes, *The Tastemakers* (New York, 1954). On blacks in World War II see Richard M. Dalfiume, *Desegregation of the U.S. Armed Forces, 1939–1953* (Columbia, 1969), and Dominic Capeci, Jr., *The Harlem Riot* (Philadelphia, 1977). An interesting collection of sources is gathered in Bernard Sternsher's *The Negro in Depression and War: Prelude to Revolution, 1930–1945* (New York, 1969). No satisfactory account of Indians in the war has been written, but see U.S. Office of Indian Affairs, *Indians in the War* (Washington, 1946), and Doris A. Paul, *The Navajo Code Talkers* (Philadelphia, 1973). The experiences of Chicanos are discussed in Manuel Servin (ed.), *The Mexican-Americans* (Beverly Hills, 1970). Much has been written on Japanese-Americans during the war including Morton Grodzins in *Americans Betrayed* (Chicago, 1949) and two works by Roger Daniels, *The Politics of Prejudice* (Berkeley, 1962) and *Concentration Camps U.S.A.* (New York, 1971).

Index